THE GRAY BIRD SINGS

THE GRAY BIRD SINGS

The Extraordinary life of

Betty Kwan Chinn

Karen M. Price, Ph.D.

THE PRESS AT CAL POLY HUMBOLDT

The Press at Cal Poly Humboldt
1 Harpst Street
Arcata, California 95521-8299
(707) 826-5602
press@humboldt.edu
press.humboldt.edu

ISBN: 978-1-962081-00-9

Developmental editing by Kyle Morgan
Layout and design by Sarah Godlin
Copyediting by Lowercase Editorial Services
Proofing by Amanda Dinscore, MLIS; Kiran Dunning; Ann Lynch, MA;
Janice Zoradi, MA

We appreciate all the photographers who have volunteered images for this
publication. If the image attribution is unlisted, it is unknown. Please contact
us if you are a photographer of one of these images, so we may attribute you
properly for future editions. If you are a photographer of one of our unat-
tributed images and wish your image to be removed from this publication,
please email the Press at Cal Poly Humboldt with the request.

Names have been changed and some details obscured to protect the identity
of Betty's clients.

"Endurance is not just the ability to bear a hard thing, but to turn it into glory."

William Barclay

"Kintsugi is the Japanese art of repairing broken pottery by mending the areas of breakage with lacquer dusted or mixed with powdered gold, silver or platinum; it treats breakage and repair as part of the history of an object, rather than something to disguise. As a philosophy, kintsugi is... an embracing of the flawed or imperfect."

Wikipedia, retrieved November 10, 2022

Table of Contents

The Betty Kwan Chinn Homeless Foundation

All royalties from the sale of this publication will go directly to the Betty Kwan Chinn Homeless Foundation. If you would like to support the Foundation and their work, please go to https://bettychinn.org/how-to-help/donations/.

For more information about donating materials, monetary donations, or volunteering, please contact the Foundation at:

Email:	bchinn@bettychinn.org
Phone:	(707) 407-3833
Location:	133 7th Street
	Eureka, CA 95501
Mailing:	P.O. Box 736
	Eureka, CA 95502

Acknowledgments

This biography was written with the help, encouragement, and support of many people. I hope that if I have inadvertently left off the name of one of the many who helped, you will know my appreciation regardless, and will forgive my oversight.

First and foremost, my thanks go to Betty, who had the courage and tenacity to tell me her story in the face of the pain of remembering, and to entrust to me the writing of that story. Lisa Bethune generously provided me access to her years of documentation of Betty's work, and also provided helpful advice as she read the manuscript. In addition, Lisa read the entire first draft manuscript with Betty, providing emotional support to Betty in the process of revisiting painful memories. Drs. Gary Deddo and Roger Newell, friends from so many stages of our lives, gifted me with their scholarship, experience in writing and publishing, and insightful advice, making this a far better manuscript. My dear friend Janice Zoradi, MA, bequeathed me with her experience as an author, and her enormous talent in editing; she corrected many mistakes, rephrased awkward sentences, and did it with great kindness. Neurosurgeon Dr. John Aryanpur generously lent me his expertise in reviewing the portions on trauma and the brain. Dr. Therese DesCamp kindly read and commented on the manuscript. Dr. Rollin Richmond, President Emeritus of Humboldt State University and a member of the Betty Kwan Chinn Foundation Board, thoroughly read and helpfully commented on the manuscript even as he was making ready to move across the country. Ann Lynch, MA, English instructor extraordinaire, provided excellent proofing. My pastor and friend, The Rev. Dr. Daniel D. London, read the manuscript with thoughtful, keen insight and gave me crucial suggestions. I am deeply grateful to all these readers.

Photographer Gary Todoroff generously gave permission for the use of his many wonderful pictures of Betty taken over the years, for which I am thankful. Kyle Morgan, Publisher at Cal Poly Humboldt University Press, along with his staff, have, with enormous skill and deep experience, graciously guided this book into final form: a deep bow of gratitude.

My husband Dan, and our son and daughter-in-law, Michael and Ella Price, were my first readers and commented on early drafts. Along with our daughter and son-in-law Heather Price Curran and Brett Curran, they provided constant encouragement and loving patience throughout the process. Our grandkids provided entertaining diversion. Finally, I am grateful to Fr. Richard Rohr and the other faculty of the Living School at The Center for Action and Contemplation, and to each of my Living School Circle Group members, who helped me to deepen to this task.

"Don't ask what the world needs. Ask what makes you come alive and go do it. Because what the world needs is people who have come alive."

Howard Thurman, *The Living Wisdom of Howard Thurman:*
A Visionary for our Time

Betty Kwan Chinn is a person who has come alive.

When Betty was seven years old, her home was destroyed and her family torn apart by the Chinese Cultural Revolution. Red Guards-paramilitary groups of students and young people organized by Chairman Mao—along with professional soldiers of the People's Liberation Army (PLA), imprisoned Betty in the village garbage dump, where she suffered constant torture. She endured for three years, until, along with three of her siblings, she made an incredibly dangerous year-long escape to Hong Kong.

Betty's ability to withstand years of torment depended partly upon inbuilt neurological protections in the human brain.

In the face of such overwhelming threats, such as those Betty experienced daily for four years, the earliest and most primitive reptilian brain takes over. An involuntary mechanism in the amygdala and hippocampus, among other locations, produces the fight-flight-freeze reaction as a survival strategy.[1] This mechanism likely helped Betty sit silently and without movement during long months when to move brought punishment. Though she felt absolute helplessness, she was also aided in her survival by the protective mechanism of dissociation, which the brain can employ during and after trauma. This protection allowed some intolerable periods of time to become remote and unfocused. As a result, the chronology and some details of events that happened to Betty cannot be perfectly reclaimed. While

---

1   Peter A. Levine, *Waking the Tiger: Healing Trauma* (Berkeley: North Atlantic Books, 1997), 85-96, 140-1.

these adaptations of the brain allow a traumatized person to endure the unendurable, the result may be that some memories are incomplete, distorted, or out of order.[2]

The effects of trauma on memory are myriad. Some of Betty's memories as recounted in this narrative are vividly recollected because of the brain's heightened alertness when the events occurred. But the brain does not encode and store memories literally, like a video recorder. Many factors shape what the brain actually encodes, stores and retrieves, and memories can be revised with re-visiting. Up to a point, the more intense and terrifying an image the more vivid may be the memory of the event because the output of stress hormones during trauma affects memory consolidation. However, if the trauma is so overwhelming as to result in "inescapable shock," the memory system may become overwhelmed and break down.[3] At those times, traumatic memories may be more likely to be retained implicitly as bodily sensations and feelings. As a result of post-traumatic stress disorder (PTSD) traumatic memories can be intrusively re-experienced as somatic sensations or bodily flashbacks. Sensory experiences including certain smells, taste, or touch can result in feelings of panic. Elevated blood pressure and heart rate, both consequencs of sympathetic nervous system activation, can be evoked by benign triggers that remind the person of the traumatic event.[4]

The early events chronicled in the first chapters, occurred when Betty was very young (from seven to twelve years of age), and therefore those events were encoded into memory before she could understand much of the political, cultural or familial context for her ostracism and torture. The innocence of some of her recollections is a glimpse into how young she truly was when they happened. When there are disparities in details, usually chronology, they derive from the "haze of trauma" already described. In those cases, I have chosen the chronology

---

2 Ibid, 208-16.
3 Antje Gentsch, Esther Kuehn, "Clinical Manifestation of Body Memories: The Impact of Past Bodily Experiences on Mental Health," *Brain Sciences* 12, no. 5 (2022): 592. https://doi.org/10.3390/BRAINSC 12050594.
4 Bessel van der Kolk, *The Body Keeps Score: Brain, Mind and Body in the Healing of Trauma* (New York: Penguin Books, 2014). 178.

that seems most likely in light of the context and other facts. The major facts of the stories are remarkably consistent. Betty's commitment to honesty is one of her strongest traits. As the chronicler of what Betty has told me, I have attempted to be faithful in documenting the story presented to me to the best of my ability.

Over the years, I have watched Betty struggle over and over for the correct word or nuance, conscientiously and completely devoted to the truth. This integrity is in fact one of Betty's most striking and consistent character traits.

~

Trauma and its effects on memory notwithstanding, this narrative is the true account of Betty's early life, and beyond. It is scar literature, or "literature of the wounded," a specifically Chinese genre which emerged in the 1970's, after Mao Zedong's death. Scar literature documents the sufferings experienced in mainland China during the Cultural Revolution, which took place from 1966 to 1976. Betty's story thus becomes a part of a larger body of literature about the horrors of that decade.

Corroborating information has been found in many historical, personal and official accounts, some of them smuggled out of China, which confirm Betty's memory of what she suffered during the Cultural Revolution. While Betty has not read any of those accounts, they have supported and echoed virtually all of her experiences, including detailed portrayals of persecution eerily similar to her own. The reports that have been written by and about other survivors of the Cultural Revolution, detail horrors that mirror what Betty experienced.[5] Virtually all the torment which Betty described has also been reported by others persecuted during the Cultural Revolution.[6]

---

5 Chen Ruoxi, *The Execution of Mayor Yin* (Bloomington: Indiana University Press, 2004), xiv.
6 Ruoxi, 2004; Feng Jicai, *Voices from the Whirlwind: An Oral History of the Chinese Revolution* (New York: Random House, 1991); Feng Jicai, *Ten Years of Madness: Oral Histories of China's Cultural Revolution* (San Francisco: China Books and Periodicals, 1996)

These now numerous documents sadly substantiate Betty's memories of her own experience. This external validation is profoundly important to Betty, who until the last decade did not know that others had experienced the kinds of torture she endured. The preponderance of documentation also alleviates her fear that she will not be believed if she tells her story.

Betty's personal family history is drawn mostly from her own experience and recollection.

Discussing the Cultural Revolution is a difficult step for many Chinese, even those now living as expatriates. The terror of the violence and persecution of that era have left them with great apprehension, and in some cases physical and psychological trauma. Many fear retribution from the Chinese government should they speak out, even decades after their escape. Others fear the shame and loss of face with their families if these sad and tumultuous events were brought to light.

Betty herself is clear that this is her story alone; these are her memories. She makes no claim to speak for her siblings, or any of her family, or any other Chinese citizen who endured the Cultural Revolution. Remembering and speaking of all of this has been an utterly painful process for Betty. Yet it has also strengthened her.

Betty possesses and embodies a deeply ingrained Christian faith, imbued with the rituals and rhythms of Catholic worship. The Eucharist is particularly meaningful to her, and has become an important part of her spiritual nurture as a "visible sign of an invisible grace."

Betty says repeatedly that she believes God spared her for her life work. She is doing what makes her come alive, and heals her.

There is a surprising power wielded by those whose heart is pure. Betty, while a flawed and imperfect human like us all, exhibits purity of heart. She evidences no hidden agenda. She wants nothing for herself, neither money nor fame. She is single-minded about her passion, which is to help the poor. One can discern no guile or self-interest in her work. This is so rare that it may be hard to believe at first, as though it must be artifice, as though really, she must want something for herself. But long observation reveals a beautiful sameness.

Betty often repeats that serving the poor has been her own healing, where she found her identity. Every person she helps adds to her wholeness. She is not tempted by money, power, acclaim, possessions or position. It is as though any receptor sites for such things were burned out of her in the garbage dump. This gives her a remarkable freedom to do her work without being distracted.

Year after year Betty remains the same simple person, doing the work she is called to do, the work her childhood suffering equipped her to do. When asked about happiness, Betty said, "Happiness you build for yourself. You can be happy no matter where you are. I appreciate my young life; if I hadn't suffered at that time it wouldn't have built the passion in my heart."[7]

Betty has gleaned through her suffering what mystics of the world religions take a lifetime of studying and contemplation to learn. She has a: "certain independence from the conditions of one's life."[8] She says, with her broad, luminous smile: "I'm free! It's not about me, it's about the homeless." Betty possesses that rare ability to acknowledge and even embrace pain, as well as awards and success, without letting them define her. She finds her joy in the daily mundane work of love.

Betty has transformed her suffering into illumination, a light which she shares with the most marginalized. Though Betty would never identify herself with such august company, she is in a long tradition of Christian contemplatives like St. Francis of Assisi, Teresa of Avila, St. John of the Cross and Teresa of Calcutta, who, like Jesus, intentionally identified with the poor.

~

I first met Betty in 2002 when she received the local Humboldt County Peacemaker Prize. By then, she already had a long history in Eureka as a beloved aide and office worker at Lafayette Elementary School. Her long work feeding the hungry was just becoming known, though she had been doing it-alone-for decades. As I began to observe

---

7 Jon Gerdemann (Director). *Joy Makers* (Motion Picture), Threesixzero Productions Pte Ltd., China, 2019.
8 James Finley, lecture at Living School Intensive, Santa Monica, CA, February 2020.

Betty's cheerful tenacity, her relentless pursuit of better ways to help the hungry, and her utter lack of self-consciousness, I wanted to know her better. We went to each other's house for dinner. Gradually we came to know one another and to develop trust.

My husband, whom Betty calls Pastor Dan, became an advocate for Betty in numerous ways. He went with her to meet the police chief whose officers had been harassing her. He and the elders of the First Presbyterian church arranged for Betty to cook out of the church's commercial kitchen. He became the first chair of the board of her foundation and a volunteer with the children's program, playing music, taking kids on sport adventures, and being a counselor at the summer camps. As the relationship between our families deepened, Betty began to share her story.

In 2008 when she received the Minerva Award from California's First Lady Maria Shriver, my husband, Dan, and I, along with others, traveled to Long Beach to see her honored. When she received the Presidential Citizens Medal in 2010, we were invited to the White House ceremony. It is one of our deepest regrets that we were not able to make that trip.

As Betty told me her story, we discussed my writing it one day. With that end in mind I took notes when we met, usually on my computer but sometimes by hand. Sometimes we met at my office, sometimes at my home. Because Betty is competent but not comfortable with written English, and her speech is accented with her native language, these face to face communications were essential. Although I am a clinical psychologist, recently retired, I was never in a professional relationship with Betty. She had help over the years from several wonderfully skilled clinicians. But my clinical experience with traumatized people gave me even more respect for the life she was living in spite of the trauma she had endured.

What she and her family had suffered was unspeakable. The woman sitting with me was emotionally marked, struggling through bouts of Post-Traumatic Stress Disorder in order to speak of what had happened, and to do what she did every day in serving the poor. Yet her essential spirit seemed unmarred. In fact, it seemed burnished by her suffering.

When I first began to write this manuscript in 2010, Betty had received a lot of public attention because of the awards she had received. Her extended family members were quite concerned and some were frightened that the attention would draw repercussions from the Chinese government. They did not want to claim relationship to Betty for fear that her acclaim would shine a spotlight on their lives, and perhaps disrupt their hard—earned stability after escaping Mao's China. Consequently, it seemed necessary to hold off on writing this story until things settled.

Ten years later, when I retired, it was finally time to write Betty's story. I felt guilty that I'd not resumed the work sooner. I had never written a book before and felt inadequate to the task of representing this incredible woman. An opportunity had emerged for a professional writer-one with extensive research and editing resources-to write her biography. Perhaps I was off the hook and would not have to risk making a fool of myself. So, I went to talk with Betty and I asked her if she still wanted me to write. I fully expected her to acknowledge my effort was now unnecessary. Instead, she said immediately, "I want you to write the God story."

With trepidation, I agreed. I wanted to be faithful to the story Betty had told me. If this book can be one small contribution to the story of Betty's life, I will be glad.

This writing is clearly mixed genre, because it is biographical but also a tribute. I have inserted reflections, quotes and interpretations in Supplemental Information sections into the story of Betty's life because her story fits into a larger context. She is part of a long spiritual lineage, and what she lives every day belongs with the legacy of those rare and brave people who have used great suffering in the service of great love.

It is the story Betty told me. It is also my reflection about the most amazing woman I have ever met. As she has so many others, she has helped me come more fully alive. Knowing her has given me a deeper understanding of our oneness with each other, and our responsibility for one another. I remain ever grateful.

Karen M. Price, Ph.D.
September 2023

Introduction

The Gray Bird

"Hope" is the thing with feathers –
That perches in the soul –
And sings the tune without the words –
And never stops – at all –

– Emily Dickinson, "'Hope' is the Thing with Feathers"

The Red Guard had tied her to a tree with a belt a short distance from the dump. Her hands were bound with rope behind her and her feet, as always, chained together. The guards tied bells to her bonds so that if she moved or tried to sit down, they would hear, and come to beat or kill her.

She understood why other children had given up and given themselves over to the escape of death. She had decided to join them. The year of torture, starvation, and exposure had worn away her will to live. She wanted to do it on her own terms, on ground that was not fouled by excrement and garbage. By using defiant disobedience, she had decided to invite the Red Guard to kill her.

So, she let her legs crumble and she slid down to the base of the small tree, bells ringing loudly. She wriggled out of the belt enough that she could lie on her back. She closed her eyes and waited, even hoped, for the guards to come with their rifles and bayonets.

But instead of the Red Guard, a small gray bird appeared. It was a common, drab little bird, perhaps a warbler. It was no mighty raptor or bird of prey, no dread carrion eater or brightly plumed beauty—just a tiny, gray, seed-and-insect-eating ordinary bird. It alit first on a branch, tipping and cocking its head as it trilled and chirped. A private avian concert for one.

Then the bird, growing bolder, landed on the girl's feet and began to lightly peck at them with its beak. She opened her eyes and, irritated, tried to kick the brash bird away; she was waiting for death and the bird was interrupting. It flew away at her movement, but came right back. This time, the presumptuous little bird hopped up the girl's legs, across her chest, and onto her shoulder. The child kept her eyes closed and tried to ignore the creature. But the bird was adamant; it began gently pecking her forehead, and then scratching with its little clawed feet near her eyes until she was forced to open them. When she did, the bird grew very still and looked at her, brown eye to brown eye. This little bird seemed to see her with an expression more like that of an inquisitive, even caring human, or some benevolent spirit, than a small winged creature. It seemed not only sentient but purposeful.

Turning away and brushing off the bird once more, the child prepared to return to thoughts of death. She watched the gray bird take wing, gracefully catching the wind. Then she closed her eyes again, sinking into the interim between life and its end. To her chagrin and amazement, the bird returned a third time almost immediately. Once again, it landed on her torso, hopped up to her shoulder, and, as though trying to rouse her rather than hurt her, began pecking and scraping, forcing her to open her eyes.

The bird stayed quietly on her shoulder, and somehow from tiny creature to tortured girl, eye to eye, a connection was made. Limbic resonance was established. She was no longer alone. The bird cocked its head as though communicating intently, as though it wanted to speak to the desolate depths of the girl. This time, she forced herself to hold its gaze.

Seeming satisfied at last, the gray bird took wing with surprising force. It caught a draft of wind and was lifted quickly, soaring powerfully. The gray bird flew directly into the sun, wings brightened to radiance. As tiny as the gray bird was, the child was surprised to find that she could see it flying into the horizon for quite some time. The little girl sat up. In an entirely unusual occurrence, the guards had failed to come. If that gray bird could fly away, maybe she too could find a way to fly out of her situation. Maybe there was hope.

She chose to live another day.

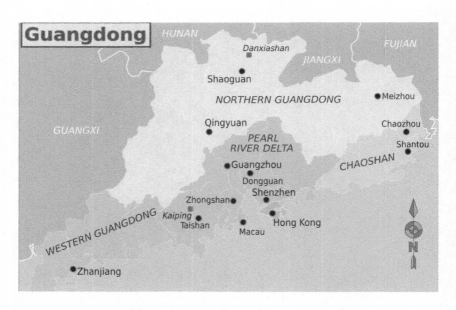

Top: Location of Guangdong province in China
(TUBS, Wikimedia Commons, September 15, 2011, https://commons.wikimedia.org.)

Bottom: A map of major cities of Guangdong Province
(Cacahuate at wts wikivoyage, PhiLiP (svg base), Shaundd (2019 modifications), Wikimedia
Commons, February 16, 2010. https://commons.wikimedia.org.)

Chapter 1

The Place Where She Began

Betty Kwan Chinn has never known her actual birth date, nor with any certainty her birth year. This is what happens when a government erases you.

The Kaiping area of Guangdong Province (formerly Canton), where Betty and her siblings were born, is also the ancestral home to many Chinese Americans and Chinese Canadians who emigrated from China beginning in the late 19th century and into the 20th. Many local Kaiping families depended upon money sent home by sons and husbands who had left for employment in the Americas and southeast Asia. In spite of the lushness of the land and the easy access to waterways that enabled trade and commerce, many impoverished Cantonese emigrants left for areas where employment was more readily available and rewarding.[1]

After surviving the hardship of Mao's Great Leap Forward (1958–1962), the Kwan family entered the early 1960s in Kaiping feeling stable and secure. The family was generationally wealthy, owning many of the village buildings and large expanses of fertile acreage and rich farming land in the moderate climate of Kaiping. Abundant rainfall and summer warmth ensured productive crops of rice, tea, and myriad lush fruits, vegetables, and flowers. Snow peas

---

1   The Kaiping area is divided into townships, districts, and villages. Betty's family home was in Chikan Township, in the Longbei District and the village of Longonc. H. Schukwing, *Kaiping Diaolou*. China, 92.

grew on trellises, and fields were planted with daikon radish, yams, oblong Chinese cabbage and round American cabbage, mushrooms, beans, and celery, among other seasonal vegetables. Rice was a staple with every meal. Yams were eaten fresh in the summer and dried for the winter. An herb garden supplied the kitchen chef. Papayas, guavas, kiwis, persimmons, apples, apricots, and plums ripened for the picking. Fragrant jasmine plants scented the home. Pigs and chickens were raised for the table.

The Kwan family was at the epicenter of a thriving and deeply connected community. They owned several restaurants in addition to the dual business of tea and rice production; many of the villagers were employed in one of the Kwan enterprises. Their property holdings were so extensive that with the birth of each new child, a building was named after them. The building named after Betty was a three-story structure of stone and white stucco, with two-story pillars in the front and a wrought-iron outdoor porch on the third floor reached from the inside by four tall, red French doors. The roof was decorated with an elaborate edifice and carvings. It was an elegant and substantial building, a metaphor for the significance of the Kwan family in Kaiping.

The main house, in which the Kwan grandparents and parents lived, and where the family meals and gatherings took place, had stood and been improved upon for generations. The house and some other buildings boasted flushing toilets with running water, which was highly unusual, even outlandish, in Kaiping at that time. This plumbing was built on the instruction of one of Betty's uncles, who had trained as an architect in the West and returned to bring his education to his ancestral home.

While ethnically Chinese, Betty's mother had been raised and educated in California, and was an American citizen. Born Tak-chui Ng (pronounced Eng), her family had emigrated when Tak-chui's father bought large tracts of farming land in the Central Valley of California, near Merced and Stockton. Along with several of her sisters, Tak-chui trained as a doctor. Her marriage to Jack Kwan—which, like many marriages within traditional Chinese families, was arranged—united two prominent families with deep roots in Kaiping. Jack was educated in Britain and trained as a dentist. He held the important role of first Kwan son after his elder brother was presumed lost in the Second Sino-Japanese War.

After their marriage, Jack and Tak-chui established themselves in the Kwan family home in Kaiping. The Drs. Kwan attempted a balancing act to bring Western ideas, along with much needed medical skills, to their conservative ancestral village. They set up a dental clinic and a medical clinic in separate adjoining buildings. Their charitable endeavors among the poor, disabled, and abandoned were well known, and both clinics were heavily utilized.

Tak-chui broke cultural norms. Because she was raised and educated in America, she had more progressive cultural values than most of her extended family and community. She was raised in a nuclear family that valued the education of its daughters as much as its sons; all were encouraged to attain professional degrees, and Tak-chui had come to value her professional life. She and her husband prioritized their daughters' education as equal to their sons'. In fact, their two eldest daughters were sent to boarding school in

The Kwan Family building named after Betty at her birth

Hong Kong before their brothers. This stood in stark opposition to Chinese tradition and the mores of Kaiping, which held that women were subservient to men and should focus on serving their husbands and raising children.

The Drs. Kwan introduced to Kaiping villagers a new and even revolutionary marital model: two educated parents, each pursuing their own professional calling, while raising a large family. This was possible because of the extensive resources at their disposal. Their Western life and training had given them new templates, which they were living out in a very conservative and traditional Chinese setting.

In a grassy open courtyard, with the church and two charity homes in the background, a large rectangular well provided water for the family. The well housing walls were painted red, with a black cupola roof and a large seamed bucket to lower into the fresh, clean water. While most villagers took their water from the river running through Kaiping, the Drs. Kwan insisted on the cleaner well water for their compound. The scientific understanding of the necessity of clean water, like the scientific understanding of disease as caused by physical organisms rather than bad luck or punishment, was part of the Western mindset that the Drs. Kwan brought to their village.

Betty's mother was especially passionate about helping the dispossessed. She established both a lepers' home and a home for abandoned blind girls on the family compound, right behind the church that grandfather Kwan had helped build. Lepers were seen as abhorrent and dangerous by the villagers, so Dr. Kwan's care and treatment of them was an aberration. At the time, lepers in China would most often be shunned and put out on the streets to die. A folk tale said that leprosy could be cured by having sex with young girls; some villagers feared the enactment of this lore, and were frightened when the lepers walked outside on the village green. They resented Tak-chui for encouraging the lepers to go outdoors for sun and exercise. Some thought that ill health and misfortune were karmically deserved, and that those lepers—many without noses and fingers and with damaged eyes—had brought their misfortune upon themselves.

Orphan girls were also common in China at that time, many of them intentionally abandoned by their families.[2] A traditional valuing of sons over daughters contributed to this practice. A daughter would become part of her husband's family upon marriage, and her parents could expect no help from her in old age. A son, on the other hand, stayed with his family and had a filial responsibility to care for elderly parents. When resources were scarce and it was difficult to feed children, sons were hence preferred at the expense of daughters.

No known studies reveal the extent of infant abandonment during this era of hardship in the Guangdong province. However, based on a study on infant abandonment in the province during the late 1980s, an analyst projected that ten thousand infants were abandoned in the province each year, 90% percent of which were female, and 22.6% disabled or deformed.[3]

One of the more common female disabilities seen by Tak-chui Kwan was blindness, including those intentionally blinded.[4] Tak-chui rescued and cared for many of these blind girls, even hiring musicians to teach them to sing so their unimpaired hearing could compensate for their lost sight. Many became skilled choir members at the church next door and some of them eventually married.

Dr. Kwan had an obstetrics specialty, delivered many babies, and was dedicated to reducing infant and maternal mortality. She convinced pregnant women not to work in the fields up until the very day they gave birth, as was the prevailing norm, but rather to rest and eat well. This medical instruction removed a needed worker from the fields for a time, angering some in the community.

As was common among households of the Kwans' status, the paternal grandmother provided a servant girl, or nanny, for each new child born into the family. These girls came from impoverished families and were

---

2 In China the terms 'abandoned' and 'orphaned' are often used interchangeably, to mean children no longer cared for by their parents (Anna High, "'Non-Legal' Orphanages and the Chinese State." China Development Brief. October 10, 2013. https://chinadevelopmentbrief.org/reports/non-legal-orphanages-and-the-chinese-state/).

3 Julie Jimmerson, "Female Infanticide in China: An Examination of Cultural and Legal Norms," *UCLA Pacific Basin Law Journal 8*, no. 1 (1990): 73. https://escholarship.org/uc/item/80n7k798.

4 Betty reported that sometimes abandoned girls would be intentionally blinded so they could not make their way back home.

at risk of abandonment, or worse, of being sold into sexual slavery or as child brides. Even as nannies in wealthy families, most were treated little better than enslaved servants, called by a number instead of their name.

As in so many things, the Kwans were different. Betty's mom accepted these children into her home as a way to help the girls out of poverty. She and Jack Kwan viewed them as extended family, calling the servant girls by their name and insisting that their children call them "sister" or "aunt." Against tradition, they allowed male and female servants to be together in the same room; and not only that, allowed them to eat together and, at times, to join the family for meals.

Betty's father had a ring made with a jade bridge and gold trusses to represent the bridge that would keep the Kwan clan connected. He then cut the jade ring in two, one half to be given to Betty at her marriage and the other half to Betty's "nanny-sister" Soon Lin at her marriage. It was her father's way of symbolizing the connection between Betty and her nanny within the family clan. In further evidence of the nannies' status within the family, when each nanny married, they were given five pieces of gold or jade jewelry as was the custom for parents to give to daughters upon marrying. The family provided ongoing financial help to these women as long as they lived.

Betty's paternal grandfather Kwan was proud of his fiery American daughter-in-law, but her grandmother Kwan was less enchanted. Both grandparents were insistent that the young Drs. Kwan have lots of children, and in doing so they pleased both Kwan grandparents. Tak-chui and Jack Kwan had ten children: four sons and six daughters.

In the family compound, the boys and girls had separate houses,

Betty's half of the jade ring provided by her father. The other half was given to Betty's "nanny-sister" Soon Lin to signify their everlasting connection.

nestled close to the main house. Each child had a room for themselves and their nanny, with a closet for hanging clothes. The family routine was firmly set. The children rose early under the supervision of their nannies. They changed into day clothes, washed their faces and brushed their teeth, and then went to the common room in their respective houses for breakfast, which was usually a bowl of rice soup. The Drs. Kwan spent the early mornings together in prayer and study. They breakfasted together, looked over their patient lists, and planned the day before the children joined them. Then the older children went to school or tutors.

Betty was the fourth daughter and the eighth child. By the time she was old enough to participate in this routine, her four eldest siblings had already gone away to Hong Kong for boarding school or university. Her father, whom the children called Papa, owned a house on the Kowloon Peninsula of Hong Kong, which his older children used as a base for their Hong Kong boarding schools, university education, and then employment, before moving to America. The eldest daughter, Faye, had already completed her education and was in America, married with a family of her own. Betty's eldest brother, Kim, had finished his education in Hong Kong and returned to Kaiping to help manage the family businesses. Kim and his wife lived in a separate house in the family compound. Elder brother Alex and elder sister Pat were also established in Hong Kong.

When the older children who were still living at home (Kathy, King, and Michael) went to their morning study, Betty, too young for formal tutoring, often took her place in a small second-floor room above the dental clinic. It had been built especially for her by her father. It had a window directly into his dental surgery, where she could see him as he worked. Betty was fascinated by the activities and rhythms of the dental surgery and her father's profession. She had a front row view of him and could observe all of his procedures, but could see only the backs of the heads of the patients in the dental chair. Shiny porcelain basins and sterilized steel dental instruments were carefully placed. Equipment not in use was kept in a glass cabinet with a sliding door. Medicine was stored in tiny jars with lids, all made of clay. There was a kitchen attached to the treatment area, where a hole in a counter dropped into a little tunnel that was used for the disposal of the used clay jars, which were regularly picked up for dumping.

During summer afternoons, her father would sometimes close the dental clinic and take Betty with him down a path that wound its way to a papaya farm. There were bamboo tables scattered on green grass under the fruit trees, where Jack and some friends regularly gathered. Someone would pick a papaya and cut it. Everyone ate the fruit with chopsticks, but since Betty was too young to handle chopsticks, she speared the fruit with one stick to get it to her mouth.

Another outing she regularly took alone with her father was to the local library. He was a man of books, and he often sat immersed in words while Betty sat quietly beside him, observing the other readers, admiring the books whose treasures were still locked to her, and longing for the day when she could read them.

When Betty's father had breaks from his dental clinic, he would sometimes take her over the nearby bridge and to one of many sets of docks, where they would buy fresh fish off the boats for the evening meal. When the family regathered in the evening, they all sat together at a long table in the main house. Everyone washed their hands before being seated. The servants served the Kwan grandparents first, then the parents and guests, and finally the children. Whatever a child took on their plate had to be eaten completely, and the children were expected to eat in disciplined silence. As girls, Betty and her sisters were schooled in quiet decorum. But Betty wanted to run, yell, play, and feel free. This behavior was acceptable for boys, but forbidden to her.

After dinner, the older children went to study. Betty was curious about the Chinese characters they were learning to write with their brushes and ink. She would ask for a pencil, which was easier to handle, and stand beside her older siblings, trying to copy what they wrote. She was a quick study and learned a number of Chinese logographic characters (hanzi) in this way.[5]

---

5 While the people in the north of China and the capital, Beijing, are Mandarin speakers, the people of south China speak Cantonese, with many local dialects. The dialect spoken in the Kwan's village was Toishan. Although this was the family's mother tongue, they spoke Cantonese as well.

When she wasn't watching her siblings study, Betty and her one-year-younger sister Wendy were taught embroidery by their grandmother Kwan. The traditional art form of Yue embroidery is characteristic of Guangdong Province and the Cantonese. It is done with a very thin needle, tight stitches, and amazing realism, usually on silk fabric. It requires enormous attention and fine motor skill, as no knots can be visible, even on the back side of the fabric. Because femininity was defined, in part, as proper, silent, and reserved, girls were allowed embroidery as their primary form of creativity and recreation. A riot of color, imagination, and action could be played out on the silk.

Betty had grown up watching her grandmother's tiny bound feet and hobbling walk. In foot binding, the four smaller toes were broken and turned under and tightly bandaged until they healed in that position. For upper-class girls in her grandmother's era, small feet were the epitome of beauty: They were seen as attractive and high status, in comparison to poor country women whose feet were not bound because they were needed to work in the fields. Betty's grandmother told her never to run, because if she was careful not to run, she too would have small feet.

In their expectations of their daughters, Betty's parents were a fusion of Western and traditional Chinese culture. They combined a behavioral mandate for quiet propriety in their girls with an insistence on the finest higher education for all of their children. Betty's childhood to this point was a highly structured, predictable, and safe cocoon. She wanted more freedom to express herself, verbally and physically, than was allowed her as a girl child. But she felt secure, nurtured, and content, with a deep sense of belonging and roots that went back many generations.

In the 1940s, during the Second Sino-Japanese War, the Kwans worked to help feed their community. All sources of outside money were prohibited from entering China; expatriates were rarely able to send essential money to their Kaiping families, and many mothers, wives, and children of the men who had left to seek work were destitute. The Kwans set up regular food distribution outside their home. Tak-chui and Jack Kwan instructed that large bamboo baskets full of rice, vegetables, and fruit be set out. The family cook stood by with his knife and chopping block to slice off pieces of pork, or to butcher a chicken. These food distributions continued on special holidays like New Year, the Mid-Autumn Mooncake Festival, and Tomb Sweeping Day (Qingming, when families clean the tombs of their departed loved ones). Expatriates from Kaiping, who could not get money to their families through normal routes, were sometimes able to send collected monies through secret channels to the Kwans for distribution.

During Mao's Great Leap Forward (1958–1962), when all farming throughout China was nationalized, the Kwans' land was confiscated, and the government ordered that all farming and distribution of food be done collectively. Citizens were organized into groups and worked communally to raise and allocate the food. The result was the complete disruption of food production across China. "The experiment ended in one of the greatest mass killings in history, with at least 45 million people worked, starved or beaten to death."[6]

Some of the Kwan family went into hiding, while others managed to organize a storehouse in which they cached as much rice from their fields as they could hide from the authorities. From there they ran an underground food distribution system. Hungry villagers came to the covert rice storage locations to fill their bowls. They were all taking an enormous risk. Helicopters from Taiwan flew overhead to drop bags of rice into the fields for their starving countrymen. However, the villagers were often too terrified of government retribution to take it for themselves, and instead turned it over to the authorities.[7]

Toward the end of this dark time, Betty's paternal grandfather, the patriarch of the Kwan family, died. There was an elaborate funeral and burial procession, in keeping with both the traditions of respect for ancestors and the status of the family as one of the most prominent in

---

6 Frank Dikotter, *The Cultural Revolution: A People's History, 1962–1976* (New York: Bloomsbury Publishing, 2016), 10.

7 The government took control of the Kwan farming land during these years, but the Kwan family technically maintained the title and deed to their property. As the Great Leap Forward faded into ignominy, landowners once again farmed their own land. Some years after the end of the Cultural Revolution, in the 1990s, Betty's eldest sister Faye returned to China with the family land titles and deeds in hand. She met with government authorities, who agreed that the Kwan family should have their land returned. However, her brothers wanted nothing to do with such a transaction and refused to engage in the process. The family let go of the ancestral home.

the province. The details of such an important event were prescribed down to the order of those walking in the procession to the graveyard. First behind the casket, carrying the incense burner, came the eldest surviving son, Jack Kwan. Protocol dictated that behind the eldest son came the wife of the deceased, then the other children, the daughters-in-law and sons-in-law, and, finally, at the very end of the long family procession, the grandchildren. Breaking with deeply held tradition, Papa carried one-year-old Betty in his arms as he followed his father's casket. The public display of physical affection was as atypical as the breaking of protocol. A scandalized village noted this aberration, and the story was told repeatedly.

There was a reason beyond paternal affection for Papa carrying Betty in his arms during the funeral procession, and for building a room for her above his dental surgery and keeping her close on his walks to the papaya grove, library, and docks. Of the Kwan children, Betty was the only child to have been openly, publicly baptized. Given local prejudices, this was a rare event. The baptism was performed when Betty was one month of age, the time of the traditional naming ceremony. It was done in a large, open-air ceremony set in a beautiful garden, on the elaborate steps leading down into the Tanjiang River. A young, Cantonese-speaking Catholic priest from Hong Kong was brought in for the occasion.

On that day, Betty was wrapped in white, which in Christianity is a sign of purity, innocence, birth, and light. In the Catholic liturgy, it is the ceremonial color for the holy days of Easter and Christmas, but in Chinese traditional culture, white is a sign of death—the color of the grave clothes in which a corpse is wrapped. To wrap a baby in white was more than unlucky, it was shocking and taboo.

Infant Betty was immersed in the river for the entire village to observe. For such a central family in the village to make a public display of the baptism of one of their children, wrapped in white, was an egregious departure from Chinese norms. Christians had been present for many hundreds of years in China, and Betty's own grandfather Kwan had helped build a church in Kaiping, but this spectacle of a baptism was something quite different. It passed beyond the threshold of local tolerance. Presumably, local Christians made baptism a private, discreet affair.

What was for Betty's mother a beautiful religious statement, marked her child for suspicious, even malevolent scrutiny. Her father's protectiveness of Betty was a way to counteract the animus villagers felt toward her. He tried to publicly display his fondness and protection for his fourth and set-apart daughter. For the most part, the generosity of the Kwan parents, freely offering their medical skills as well as food and employment, created goodwill among the villagers. It was more than enough to offset any suspicion that was aroused by their lapse into Western ways and their departure from traditional norms.

Until it wasn't.

Supplemental Information

Kaiping Architecture

The Kaiping area is famous for its elaborate, fortified tower houses, which were often built with funds sent back to Kaiping by expatriate Chinese husbands and sons. There are at least 1,800 of these fortress-like stone buildings, called dialou, in the Kaiping area; some of them have been designated as UNESCO World Heritage Sites.[8] These towers represent an amalgamation of Chinese and Western influence and architecture, speaking to the impact of the westernized émigrés who were sending home funds with which to erect them.

Yunhuan Lou and Qiuanjulu Mansion in Zili Diaolou Village, Tangkou Township, Kaiping, Guangdong, China (Stefan Fussan, Wikimedia Commons, October 6, 2016. https://commons. wikimedia.org/)

---

8 "Kaiping Diaolou and Villages," UNESCO World Heritage Convention, 2007, https://whc.unesco.org/en/list/1112/.

Female Infanticide

The practice of female infanticide in China has a history of more than two thousand years.[9] This custom, while illegal, continued during the time the Drs. Kwan practiced, and has been documented since the Qin dynasty (255–206 BC).[10] Then, and in recent centuries, scarce resources and valuing boys more than girls were likely primary causes.[11]

Religious traditions both contributed to and inhibited the practice of infanticide. While in Buddhist tradition, a handicap was seen as evidence of a crime in a past life, thus justifying death, there was a counter-balancing Buddhist thought that it was bad karma to allow a child to die, and good karma to save them. Being born female was a deficit in comparison to the value placed on male infants. This religious tension of competing principals encouraged the saving of at least some abandoned infants, and many Buddhist nunneries served as drop-off points for unwanted female infants.[12] Historically, many Christian missionaries, Buddhist nuns, and others rescued unwanted female children and established foundling homes and orphanages to care for them.

9 D.E. Mungello, *Drowning Girls in China: Female Infanticide since 1650* (Lanham, MD: Rowman & Littlefield, 2008), 5.
10 Infanticide was also practiced throughout Europe in antiquity; both Plato and Aristotle spoke of it. Matteo Ricci (1552–1610) wrote of it in his travels as a founder of the Jesuit China Missions.
11 Jimmerson, "Female Infanticide in China," 1990.
12 Mungello, *Drowning Girls in China*, 10.

Chapter 2

The Cultural Revolution

"If you are neutral on situations of injustice, you have chosen the side of the oppressor."
-Desmond Tutu, *Oxford Essential Quotations*

"No matter how noble the objectives of a government, if it blurs decency and kindness, cheapens human life, and breeds ill will and suspicion—it is an evil government."
– Eric Hoffer, *The True Believer*

Into this flawed Eden slithered a snake: Mao Zedong's Cultural Revolution. The roots of the upheaval of the Cultural Revolution began decades earlier when a long civil war, which was intermittent between 1927 and World War II, flamed into an all-out conflagration in 1946. The Chinese Nationalist Party (also called the Kuomintang, or KMT), led by Chiang Kai-shek, had long held off the upstart Chinese Communist Party (CCP), led by Mao Zedong. The KMT benefited from American support due to its democratic leanings. But in 1949, the CCP won a decisive victory and Mao Zedong became Chairman Mao. Chiang Kai-Shek and his followers fled to the island of Taiwan, where they established the Chinese Nationalist Party in exile.

When Mao took power in mainland China, the nation had been battered by a long series of wars and upheaval, and its economic and governmental systems were in disarray. Mao sought to unify his people around communist ideals. Frustrated by the country's slow progress and desperate to "reset" China along communist lines, Chairman Mao instituted the Great Leap Forward, which resulted in the Great Famine. Between 1959 and 1962, tens of millions of people starved to death.[1] In an attempt to recover from this enormous failure and consolidate his power, Mao presided over yet another disaster four years later: the Cultural Revolution.

In 1966, he began to purge the CCP of revisionists and reassert his authority. He organized students in their teens and twenties and whipped them up to the intensity of revolutionary fervor and ideological purity that had brought about the CCP's victory twenty years earlier. Mao's slogans, "To rebel is justified" and "Bombard the headquarters," became rallying cries. Mao incited the youth to destroy "class enemies" and sanctioned them to attack anyone accused of capitalist or bourgeois leanings. These enemies came to include many high-ranking officials in his own CCP, whom Mao saw as competitors.

In the summer of 1966, Mao gathered twelve million of these students, known as the Red Guard, in Tiananmen Square. From there, the Red Guard were provided free train travel and accommodations to spread the revolution all over China.[2] Within a year, the Cultural Revolution had spread its contagion from the capital city of Beijing to the Mandarin-speaking north, and then to the Cantonese-speaking south.

Once begun, the Cultural Revolution could not easily be contained; within a year it had spread to the southern borders of China, including Guangdong Province and Kaiping. Nobody and no place went untouched. Because the "enemy" categories were so fluid and ambiguous, and because the young people charged with wreaking mayhem against those enemies were so suddenly empowered and unrestrained, atrocities occurred everywhere and against an indiscriminate swath of citizens.

Eventually, Mao grew alarmed and was forced to mobilize his highly trained military, the People's Liberation Army (PLA), to restrain the youth of the Red Guard and disperse them to the rural countryside. The PLA continued alongside the Red Guard to carry out the destruction

---

1 Kent Wong, *Swimming to Freedom* (New York: Abrams Press, 2021), 55.
2 Dikotter, *The Cultural Revolution*, 106, 108.

mandated by the Cultural Revolution in a more disciplined but equally brutal way.

~

The Cultural Revolution targeted specific groups for annihilation, known as the Five Black Categories. These categories included landlords, rich peasant farmers, counter-revolutionaries (including those who had supported the KMT and Chiang Kai-shek), bad elements (which included those who were cultured, religious, educated, professional, and wealthy), and rightists (which included intellectuals within the CCP who favored capitalism over collectivism). Anyone with close ties to the West, and especially America, which had supported the KMT, was especially endangered. Members of the Five Black Categories were subject to everything from the loss of jobs and homes to imprisonment and being "struggled against" in mass gatherings that sometimes escalated to torture or even murder.

The Kwan family would have heard rumblings of the Cultural Revolution from its inception in the north in 1966—and, given their position and history, they fit into more than one of the Five Black Categories. However, they did not appear too alarmed for their family's safety. The Kwan family had survived the Great Leap Forward, and both of Betty's parents had survived the civil war and the communist revolution. Perhaps they felt that their service to the poor and needy would exempt them from the onslaught against the privileged. Or perhaps they thought that being in the south insulated them from the worst of the atrocities.

However, the Kwan family should have been more worried for a number of reasons. The "class enemy" categories were so vaguely defined that they could, and did, include almost anyone. Mao continually changed the parameters of these categories, sometimes week to week, sowing mass confusion and paranoia.[3] The features and accomplishments that had once distinguished the Kwan family—such

---

3 Dikotter, *The Cultural Revolution*, 183–186.

as bringing modern plumbing, medical and dental care, and Western ideas to Kaiping—soon began, first subtly and then menacingly, to make them targets in a quickly deteriorating political landscape.

Both Drs. Kwan were professional intellectuals educated in the West. They were wealthy, managing large tracts of land, properties, and businesses. In addition, Betty's mom was an American citizen, and since the American government recognized and supported the exiled Chinese government in Taiwan, this made her an enemy of the state.

The Kwan family was also Catholic. In a society where Chinese traditional religion combined local customs with Buddhism, Taoism, and Confucianism, they were religious outliers. What's more, Tak-chui was overt in her social and religious convictions. In spite of her many acts of charity, she was perceived as aggressive, especially about her religion. If Tak-chui was perceived as being insensitive to Chinese rituals and traditions and accused of "pushing" Christianity as she had learned it in America, it may have inflamed historical tensions already at a boiling point between the two religious cultures.

But there was yet another reason why Tak-chui was vulnerable to political attack: her birth family, Ng,[4] supported Chiang Kai-shek and his Chinese nationalist government in exile in Taiwan. Tak-chui's parents and grandparents had been close friends with Chiang Kai-shek's mentor and the founder of the Chinese Nationalist Party, Sun Yat-sen (1866–1925).[5] Sun Yat-sen founded the pro-democracy Chinese Nationalist Party in 1919 and remained a hero to those who supported democracy over communism. When Chiang Kai-shek and his nationalist KMT party lost the civil war to Mao and his CCP in 1949, Tak-chui's Ng family remained financially and morally supportive of Chiang Kai-shek and the KMT, making them an enemy to Mao.

Though less an outlier in his community, Dr. Jack Kwan was also a target in his own right. Besides his Western education and being a member of the wealthy landed class, he was a capitalist, owning businesses that employed many people. While Jack's Christianity was

4   Tak-chui's only nephew was hidden in the Sun family home on the island of Macao for the duration of the Cultural Revolution.
5   Y.C. Wang, "Sun Yat-Sen, Chinese Leader." July 20, 1998. Encyclopedia Britannica: https://www.britannica.com/biography/Sun-Yat-sen.

not as overt as his wife's, the Kwan family was Christian-identified: his father helped build the white steepled church in the village. Jack also had deep ties to America, an object of hatred during the Cultural Revolution—a common chant during this time was "Death to America." Not only was he married to an American, he was married to an American with strong KMT ties. Jack also had many extended family members living in America, including his daughter Faye and youngest brother, George. Altogether, there could hardly be a stronger indictment of the Kwan family in the eyes of Mao's enforcers.

The villagers' suspicions and concerns about the Kwan family, nascent and subdued until this point, were gaining momentum. The Kwan family had modern Western innovations in their home, they cared for lepers and blind girls in the family compound, they removed women in late pregnancy from the fields, they upended class and gender hierarchy with their servants, they were wealthy and educated, they had family members who lived in America, and they were overtly Christian. These were all sources of wariness among the villagers. Night was falling.

Supplemental Information

Mao Zedong

At this time, Mao was approaching seventy-three and had lived a life of relative luxury, isolated from people and the broader world, except for his numerous young female companions.[6] He was an aging man, bent on purging competitors and callously ordering mass killings to subdue the populace. He had lost touch with the common people of his country and the core of his communist ideals. "At the peak of his power, Mao had drifted away from Chinese reality."[7] His health was failing, as he suffered from congestive heart failure and also developed muscle weakness and speech problems.[8] In 1974, he was diagnosed with amyotrophic lateral sclerosis (ALS). He died in September 1976 after several heart attacks. The Cultural Revolution was the natural, calamitous extension of many years of a "cult of personality" dictatorship, where dissent was brutally punished. Mao used economic and social disruption, mass campaigns, and ruthless purges to eliminate anyone who threatened his absolute power. "The Cultural Revolution then, was about an old man settling personal scores at the end of his life."[9] Mao's earlier writings were reduced to the propaganda slogans of "The Little Red Book" of Mao quotations, which were wielded and used like holy scripture by the Red Guard. "Mao himself never wrote a single comprehensive analysis of what he intended to achieve by the Cultural Revolution or of how he expected it to proceed."[10] Many of the tortures perpetrated on class enemies had already been used and refined during the Great Leap Forward. Mao was repurposing old strategies to destabilize the populace and make them more compliant.

6   Jonathan Spence, *Mao Zedong: A Life* (New York: Penguin Books, 2006), 155.
7   Timothy Cheek, *Mao Zedong and China's Revolutions: A Brief History with Documents* (Boston: Bedford/St. Martins, 2002), 30.
8   Spence, Mao Zedong, 172–78.
9   Dikotter, *The Cultural Revolution*, xiii.
10 Spence, 168.

Ancestor Veneration

Veneration of ancestors is central to Confucianism, and has strongly shaped Chinese culture and morality. In traditional Chinese culture, including Christian Chinese culture, filial piety is sacrosanct and is expressed in a variety of rituals for the dead throughout the year. Chinese traditional religions maintain that the dead ancestor, if not properly cared for, will become a "hungry ghost," or gui, free to attack anyone in the community. There is also a deeply ingrained belief that an afterlife is experienced through one's descendants in a sort of biological continuance. Many Chinese people see proper funeral rites, burial, and the annual rituals as the highest duty of children. These traditions inform their family structure. Given this context, it is clear why Betty's baptism ceremony where the infant was wrapped in "grave clothes" would have appalled the sensibilities of a traditional community.

The tolerance of the Chinese Catholic Church for allowing ancestor rituals had created a tense but workable balance between Chinese Catholic Christianity and traditional religion and rituals. Since 1939, under Pope Pius XII, the Catholic Church began to allow Chinese followers to worship Jesus as well as perform the traditional rites for their ancestors. The Papal decree established that performing rituals for one's relatives was not idolatry but was a way of honoring one's ancestors and so allowed by the Catholic Church."[11]

The 1949 Communist Revolution resulted in the expulsion of foreign missionaries, which forced the Chinese Church to take on a more national leadership and identity. Since all religious expression was suspect, the Church began to go underground, where in large part it remains today.[12] It was not only Christians who were persecuted during the Cultural Revolution; all overtly religious people, whether Buddhist, Taoist, Christian, or Muslim, were considered "counter-revolutionaries." Temples, shrines, mosques, and churches were

11 Jan Olav Smit, Pope Pius XII, London, 1951, 186–187.
12 Ian Johnson, *The Souls of China: The Return of Religion After Mao* (United States: Pantheon Books, 2017), 16–18; Liao Yiwu, *God Is Red: The Secret Story of How Christianity Survived and Flourished in Communist China* (New York: HarperCollins, 2011), viii.

destroyed with equal ferocity. To a movement that rejected any power greater than Maoism, they were all targets.

Chapter 3

Night Falls

"Nothing forces us to know what we do not want to know
except pain."
– Aeschylus

"Dignity is as essential to human life as water, food, and oxygen. The
stubborn retention of it, even in the face of extreme physical hardship, can
hold a man's soul in his body long past the point at which the body should
have surrendered it."
– Laura Hillenbrand, *Unbroken: A World War II Story
of Survival, Resilience, and Redemption*

By early 1967, when Betty was about seven years old, the Cultural Revolution was stirring in Guangdong Province. By mid-summer of that year, it was full-blown. Just three weeks after the birth of Betty's baby sister, word came via whispers in their social network that the Kwan family was soon to be denounced. Danger was upon them.

A seeming underestimation of their peril had left them unprepared for the crisis engulfing them. In the frenzied hours after word came of an impending raid, Jack Kwan made a run for his house in Hong Kong to prepare for the rest of the family to join him. Betty's mom, the planner of the family, arranged to immediately send two of her husband's elder sisters to the Hong Kong house. It seemed that it might still be possible for them all to escape to Hong Kong with some semblance of their lifestyle and dignity.

On a summer evening in 1967, Jack filled a bucket with gold coins to pay the fisherman who had agreed to take him to Hong Kong. They would row down the Tanjiang River to the Pearl River, then on to the South China Sea and across to Hong Kong. Jack took nothing else with him, except, at the last moment, Betty. She did not even have time to put on her shoes, so quickly did he pick her up and run for the door.

She rode on her father's back for the miles to the fishing dock where the boat awaited them. He told her she was not to drink any water and would have to endure thirst because there would be no toilet facilities for a long while on the river. Jack was a tall man, and broad. She loved the feeling of being carried by her beloved Papa, the strong warmth of his back and the tight grasp of his hands holding her secure. She always felt safe in his presence; the sense of his special care for her permeated her heart. She knew that as long as she was with her father, she would be safe. This unexpected adventure with him to the far docks was quite unusual—he had never taken her this far from home before—but it was also exciting. She trusted him completely.

When they arrived at the dock, it was deep night. The moon reflected on the water. Her father guided her to a sampan, a common Chinese fishing boat. The man-powered rowboat was no more than 14.5 feet long, and had a small shelter built in the middle and rough cooking implements in the stern. Her father quickly exchanged clothes with one of the two fishermen, transforming himself from a gentleman professional into a modest fisherman in a few moments. The fisherman with whom he made the trade snuck away. Betty was stowed in a box, a wooden storage bench with a hinged top that was underneath the shelter in the middle of the sampan. She was told to remain silent; she stretched out fully in the dark, warm space. Soon she heard voices and the rocking of the boat as another person, a large person, came on board. She was puzzled; Papa had not mentioned that they were waiting for another passenger, and the tiny boat was already at capacity.

Papa then lifted the lid of the box and told Betty to get out. She saw the other man that had come on board, but she did not immediately see his face. She gave her father a questioning look, but obeyed him as he told her to hop back up on the dock and unwind the anchor rope from the stanchion. She did as she was told, her back to the boat as she unwound the coiled rope from around its anchor. Suddenly the end of the rope was pulled from her hands as the boat took off. She turned around to see her father and the fisherman rowing madly, Papa's back to her. The other gentleman would not meet her eyes, but she recognized him as Mr. Sun, an old family friend who was called Uncle Sun by the Kwan children. He had left China years ago to study at Harvard University in America. He had then settled in Hong Kong, though his parents remained in mainland China. She knew he had recently come back to mainland China with his family to celebrate his mother's birthday. She saw him climb into a longer box built into the side of the boat.

Utter devastation crushed the breath from her. Confusion, disorientation, fear, and wild pain. Why was Papa leaving her? What had she done wrong? For a few moments she considered throwing herself into the water to try to follow the boat, but she had never learned to swim. The water was deep, dark, and threatening, and the boat was pulling away with frightening speed.

She stood numbly on the dock watching her father leave and felt her reality crumble. Her limbs were blocks of stone, her breathing rapid and shallow. Waves of nausea gripped her. The shock felt like a physical blow to her body. The ground under her feet had shifted, and there was no way to regain balance. This rejection could not be reconciled with all she had known of her Papa before. This loss of innocence and broken trust changed something in Betty forever.

She didn't know how she made her way back home, barefoot and alone. She only knew that the moon was shining, and the father who had carried her against all custom at his own father's funeral, who had made a special room just so she could be safe, who always kept her close by his side, had abandoned her. When she limped back into the family house, it was getting light. The rest of the family were surprised to see her. They had assumed she and her father were safely en route to Hong Kong. She did not know how to explain what had happened; shame and confusion and hurt burned in her. It would be many years before she learned the tragic story of Papa's choice.

The night after Betty's sad return from the docks, the Red Guard, joined by soldiers from the PLA, burst into the Kwan home. It was late at night and the family was sleeping. The Red Guard had gathered a large group of neighbors and other villagers to join in the destructive denunciation and "public criticism" (Fengqiao) of the family.[1]

The crowd gathered outside the house, screaming and attacking with every insult they could find. Villagers who harbored suspicion and jealousy toward the Kwan family likely felt justified in their abuse. Fear of being associated with "counter-revolutionaries" and "bad elements" kept them there, willing to surrender loyalty and decency to preserve their own lives.

The members of the mob were victims in their own way, held in the madness of a world turned upside down. Anyone thought to harbor sympathy for those being denounced was suspect; everyone had to join enthusiastically in the verbal abuse lest they be marked themselves. It was not uncommon for a person to come under suspicion and be made to join the company of the tormented simply because they were not wholehearted enough in their denunciation.

In the absurdity of those days, people were denounced and their lives crushed for a wrong word or a chance encounter. A single report from anyone was all it took for the nightmare to begin. Victims often had no idea why they were being singled out, and no explanation was given. Friends or family members became enemies from one day to the next. In that climate, even the courageous became cowards, as people tried to protect their children, spouses, and elderly parents.[2] Communist ideals were shattered in the desperation of self-protection.

The Red Guard were youth aged fifteen to twenty, including both young men and women. They tended to be local, and in the south, they spoke Cantonese. The soldiers of the PLA who joined the Red Guard at the Kwan house that night, however, had been sent from the north and spoke Mandarin. They were professional soldiers, trained and equipped. As the Red Guard and the PLA entered the house that

---

1 Massimo Introvigne, "Fengqiao Experience: The CCP Revives a Maoist Terror Strategy," *Bitter Winter*, August 13, 2020, 1.

2 Feng Jicai, *Voices from the Whirlwind: An Oral History of the Chinese Revolution* (New York: Random House, 1991) 40, 58–9, 94, 126, 160.

mid-summer night, they went room to room, grabbing and beating each family member, then harshly tying their hands behind them while screaming, "Death to America! Long live Mao Zedong!"

They systematically shattered each light bulb, filling the grand house with the sharp tinkle of breaking glass and coating the floors in a fine film of pulverized silica. Each family member was beaten with long pieces of knotted, whip-like rope, then kicked with heavy-soled leather boots. A member of the PLA kicked Betty in the tailbone with such force that it was likely broken.

Only one grace was given: the nannies, members of the family since each child's birth, were set free, as were the cook and other servants. These workers were seen as "victims" of the capitalist Kwan family and were not imprisoned. The nanny of Betty's six-year-old sister, Wendy,

Betty (standing) and her sister Wendy around 1966

begged to take her charge with her. She was refused. Regardless, Wendy managed to escape and hide in a chicken coop that night. Wendy was later rescued by a family friend, Mr. Ying, who arranged for her concealment and care in various safe houses in the capital city of Guangzhou, about seventy miles away.

The eldest son of the family, Kim, and his newly pregnant wife, lived in a separate house on the compound. They were also rounded up and brought to join the rest of the family.

When all family members had been bound, they were marched outside to the frenzied invectives of the crowd. Composed of their neighbors, former friends, and even distant relatives, the crowd gave themselves over to the political demands of the moment. They screamed and yelled and threw rocks at the Kwan family. One of the distant relatives who participated in the denunciation later said it was a matter of survival.

Betty stood outside with her family, shivering in terror and pain. She heard the yelling of the crowd, the sounds of people hitting her family with rocks and soldiers beating them with rope, and she froze into utter stillness.

From the midst of the mob, Betty heard her malediction shouted aloud for the first time: "Devil Child." The Red Guard were jeering at her and yelling it in her face. Her tormentors fashioned a wooden sign upon which they wrote with white paint in Chinese characters, *I am a Devil Child*. It was fastened around her neck with wire.[3]

Hanging a sign around a prisoner's neck as punishment was common during the Cultural Revolution. Many who were denounced were forced to wear self-critical and humiliating signs identifying them

---

3 The mogwai, or demons, are associated with the ghosts of non-family members who take retribution on the living who caused them pain. Some Chinese people make a sacrifice of burned money so that these mogwai are provided for in the afterlife. To call Betty a Devil Child was to impute to her the dark power of the vengeful dead who could malignantly affect the fate of the living. In the context of a traditionally superstitious Chinese society, some feared that Betty's public baptism had actually caused her to be enthralled by a devil, making her a being of malign power. But it is quite possible that the sign Betty was forced to wear saved her life. Those who guarded her were happy to torture her, and while that brutality could well have led to her death, the guards did not appear willing to take her life directly for fear of the consequences.

as "capital roadists" or "counter-revolutionaries," or some other form of newly minted criminality.[4] Once Betty wore this sign, no one was allowed to speak to her, under penalty of imprisonment. She was not allowed to address anyone or to look them in the eye.

During the night of the raid, Betty's mom, being an American citizen, was accused by the crowd of poisoning the community with Western thought and language. She was brutally beaten and taken to a prison outside town. At one point, Betty's paternal grandmother was thrust forward to be denounced. One of her distant relatives ran forward and began to savagely beat her.

Betty's grandmother was attacked for having Western-educated sons, and because her youngest son, George, lived in the United States. The mob launched slogans, rhetoric, and abuse against the family, throwing rocks, kicking, hitting, spitting, and taunting, until finally even such seductive mass hysteria grew tiring and the soldiers took each family member to their imprisonment.

Betty did not know where any of her siblings or her mother or grandmother were taken that night. She did not know what happened to her infant sister, who was still known as child number Ten as her naming ceremony had not yet occurred. Betty was separated from all of them. Her feet were bound with rope, her hands tied tightly behind her back. The sign was heavy around her neck, the wire cutting into tender skin. Thus hobbled, she was marched, tripping and falling while being dragged and beaten, to the community garbage dump in the outskirts of the village. When she tripped, the guard pulled her up by the rope between her hands, wrenching her shoulders out of their sockets. As she stumbled along, she heard the mocking voice of a teenage boy behind her. She knew he was one of the Red Guard and not the PLA because he spoke Cantonese. He was taunting, "Where is your God now? He cannot help you. No one can help you."

In arranging the baptism that resulted in Betty's label as a Devil Child, Tak-chui was attempting to honor her Catholic faith. What was

---

4 Dikotter, *The Cultural Revolution*, 60–63, 75; Wen Chihua, *The Red Mirror: Children of China's Cultural Revolution* (Boulder, CO: Westview Press, 1995), 160; Jicai, *Voices from the Whirlwind*, 85.

for Tak-chui a beautiful and holy religious rite instead put her fourth daughter at risk. Only too late did she realize her mistake.

The swell of approbation that flowed from this early event in Betty's life may also have been exacerbated by the human tendency to find a scapegoat to blame for misfortune or conflict. Mao had of course done this on a grand scale, diverting attention from his failed policies and blaming a wide variety of people for the suffering of the populace, who had only recently recovered from a great famine.

By turning the young, the impressionable, and the less powerful against those who represented traditional forms of power (the landed, the educated, the cultured, and the wealthy), Mao redirected the nation's hostility and blame. In microcosm, Betty became a scapegoat for her community. She was blamed and ostracized as a Devil Child, which united others in common condemnation.[5]

---

5 For a further exploration of this view of the scapegoat, see: René Girard, *The Scapegoat* (Boston: Johns Hopkins University Press, 1986).

Chapter 4

Life in the Garbage Dump

"Here is the world. Beautiful and terrible things will happen.
Don't be afraid."

– Frederick Buechner, *Beyond Words:*
Daily Readings in the ABC's of Faith

After being dropped on the ground in the garbage dump and told not to move, all that Betty could think of was the strange fact that nature went on. How could the insects keep going about their business when her world had ended? How could beauty continue to exist in the face of such ugliness? She heard the refrain of crickets and saw frogs jumping sprightly, croaking out their raucous melody. She saw the luminescence of the moon on dragonfly wings before dawn.

When the sun rose, Betty's eyes were so swollen from the beatings that she could not open them. Until the swelling receded, she was blind. Her tailbone was in exquisite pain. Her hair, face, and pajamas were caked with blood and dirt. She became familiar in those first few days with things wholly unknown to her before. She was afraid, she was in pain, she was thirsty, she was hungry, and she was alone.

Raised in a large family with her own nanny and siblings, aunts, uncles, and cousins always around, she had never been alone. Her sense of self was deeply embedded in her relationships with others.

Being cut off suddenly and violently from the network of her family was a psychological amputation. She was disoriented, physically and mentally, and in shock.

Rules in the garbage dump at the edge of town were quickly established. Betty was not to talk to anyone, ever. She was never to look at anyone, keeping her head bowed and her eyes cast down. She was not to move. She was to obey orders and remain tied; escape attempts would result in a beating or worse. There were four or five other children relegated to the dump, but there was no possibility of forming a "community of crisis" among them, or even attempting to find some fragment of humanity in the guards. The children were not allowed to look at each other, speak, or make physical contact. They had some sense of each other's presence and location, but without eye contact, talking, or touch, no human connection could develop. As children died, others took their place.

The dump was guarded both by soldiers of the PLA and members of the Red Guard. The transplanted PLA soldiers were more intimidating in their uniforms and heavy boots and had little understanding or sympathy for people from the south. The Red Guard were more like enthusiastic cheerleaders for Mao; they seemed to have little training or competence. The PLA guards stood behind the children so as not to be seen or identified, but the young members of the Red Guard did not seem to care about being seen.

Beyond the utter isolation, Betty was tormented by thirst and hunger. The guards provided neither food nor water. The guards cooked rice in front of their young prisoners, and the smells were an affliction beyond bearing. Her stomach hurt all the time. She begged for food and was laughed at. Once, a guard responded to her pleas by putting a little rice in a can as though to offer it to her. But the can had no bottom; the spoonful of rice dropped onto the foul ground. He laughed at Betty's dismay.

During this time of starvation, Betty developed a fantasy. In her vision, she would one day be so wealthy that she could afford a feast for all the poor. She vowed to herself that she would serve them on the finest porcelain and no one would go hungry.

The PLA and Red Guard watched the garbage dump children around the clock. If they were caught moving, they were beaten or made to chew rocks until their teeth broke. Most of Betty's teeth were soon ruined. Betty was often made to sit cross-legged, her hands bound behind her, with her head lowered. A rope was tied around her neck and held by a guard sitting behind her. If she moved, the guard tugged the rope until she choked.

It was only during the dead of night when the guards fell asleep that Betty discovered she could hobble to the little creek that ran by the dump and get a drink. She managed this by pulling her bound hands under her feet and in front of her body so she could dip them in the brackish, dirty water. The area was muddy and her feet sank into the muck, making it difficult to keep her balance and get in and out without falling. This nightly quest to alleviate her maddening thirst was dangerous. The first time she attempted it, she forgot to return her hands to their initial position behind her back. After a severe beating, she never forgot again. At some point the rope around her feet was exchanged for a chain. One day a guard tested the bayonet of his gun on Betty's foot, making a deep, scarring gash.

The composition of the dump was mainly dirt and human and animal waste. There were rarely any edible scraps. In desperation, this child of privilege learned to eat dirt, animal carcasses, animal waste, leaves—when she was lucky enough to get them—and any insect or reptile that got close to her. Once in a great while, at night, she was able to catch a small fish in the creek. Frogs, beetles, and other insects, as well as small snakes, became life-saving calories. During the hot, humid summer days she would sweat through her thin pajamas. They dried stiff, and the salt left in the fabric provided her a bit of comfort when she licked it.

The PLA guards would often defecate in a rusted tin can and force the children to eat the excrement. Every other day they would urinate into the can and force the children to drink it. This was the prisoners' only consistent hydration. Betty was never free from the stench of waste; the whole dump reeked of it. She felt permeated within and without by foulness.

Days melded together into weeks and months and still Betty lived. Her mind and emotions shut down in self-preservation, creating a numb void.

She lived in fragmentary moments, like worn snapshots. During growing seasons, she was taken to haul water buckets from the creek to the crops in the fields. She was also, for a brief time, taken to a labor camp. The camp was at a higher elevation where the nights were colder, and there were no blankets or pads on which to sleep. She carried full buckets of water balanced on a bamboo stick to the rice fields, from sunup to sundown. She was beaten with a rope if she walked too slowly. But this was a better existence than the garbage dump, because she was given half a yam and a bowl of watery rice soup each day. Her small and weak frame made her of little help in the rice fields, and she was often sick and crying for her mom. Inevitably, she was taken back to the garbage dump.

The verbal abuse, physical violence, and severe deprivation opened a door into isolation, cruelty, and pain. Had she known how long it would be before she was free of the garbage dump, she could not have borne the knowledge. Already, she could barely recall that her former life of abundance had existed. The little girl Betty had been was gone.

~

Betty learned not to defy the PLA soldiers' orders when a fellow garbage dump prisoner, a boy, refused to eat human waste. The soldiers put the defiant boy in the chicken coop near the dump and ordered the children to watch. They doused him with gasoline until he was drenched in the acrid liquid. Then a guard lit a match and threw it. The boy was quickly engulfed in flames, screaming in pain and writhing as he burned to death in front of the terrified children. His skin burned off and his face turned bright pink as the muscle tissue was revealed, his face frozen in an expression of agony. The smell of gasoline and scorching flesh permeated the air. The lesson was clear: to disobey even the most onerous instruction was to invite a painful death.

The guards seemed to welcome reasons to torment the children. They placed no value of any kind on their lives. The Red Guard had been told that these "enemies of the people" were dogs, not humans. Dehumanizing their enemies allowed the soldiers to treat them despicably without feeling guilt or shame. A large part of a generation of Chinese teens became Red Guard, suspending their consciences to engage in the cruelties Mao and his Cultural Revolution required of them.

~

Constantly thirsty, hungry, in pain, lonely, and frightened, Betty nevertheless found the will to survive while many of the children around her died. She clung to some internal resilience and sense of goodness, though she could no longer see or feel it. That is, until the day her will to live crumbled, and she decided to provoke a guard into killing her. Then the gray bird came.[1]

That little bird broke through Betty's despair and reminded her that goodness had not completely abandoned her.

The gray bird stayed long enough, making eye contact with Betty in its steadfast, sentient way, that by the time it took flight for the last time, Betty felt a stirring of improbable joy. When it took wing with surprising power, she felt a glimmer of hope. The small creature's very aliveness was a reminder that darkness was not complete. It was enough for her to dream that she too might fly away and escape her prison. She decided not to give up that day. And for some unknown reason, the guards never came to punish her. While a tormented child, Betty learned that hope can persist.[2] She remembered this little bird often as a personal icon of hope, sent to her in her darkest time.[3]

1 The full story about the gray bird can be found in the introduction.
2 "In the depths of winter, I finally learned that within me there lay an invincible summer," from Albert Camus, "Return to Tipasa," *Lyrical and Critical Essays* (New York: Vintage Books, 1970), 169.
3 Another survivor of torture and inhumanity wrote, "... everything can be taken from a [person] but one thing: the last of the human freedoms—to choose one's attitude in any given set of circumstances, to choose one's own way," from Viktor Frankl, *Man's Search for Meaning: An Introduction to Logotherapy* (New York: Simon & Schuster/ Touchstone, 1984), 75.

On that day, a young, small Betty made the first of many such choices, deciding that it was worth surviving for some hope of a future.

~

When a child in the dump succumbed to deprivation and abuse, their body was left for a few days to bloat, decay, and attract flies, further terrorizing the young prisoners. With bound hands and feet, the surviving children could not brush the flies away from their face, ears, nose, and mouth. The nights became colder as fall yielded to winter, offering some relief from the flies but introducing constant cold. With no insulating body fat, Betty was shaking most of the time. Summer pajamas with their light cotton bottoms and three-quarter sleeves, now tattered and worn, offered little protection against the elements to which Betty was exposed twenty-four hours a day.

After the guards fell asleep, Betty would squeeze herself under the piles of garbage and dirt and waste as some protection against the frigid night air. She had to sneak out of the layers before dawn or risk a beating if caught. Smoke was always rising from the garbage, and it was warm. It is likely that the high level of compost and waste resulted in bacterial fermentation and combustion in that pile, heating it enough to provide unexpected comfort to a cold child. During the rainy months, though, the pile would become so heavy that she could barely breathe under the weight when she crawled under it.

Even amid such deprivation, the pain of rejection in her heart was perhaps greater than her physical pain. Why had Papa left her? Why had her mother not arranged for all of them to escape? Some of her extended family still lived in the village. Why did they not help? Betty was completely and totally alone. Seeing that no one would help her, Betty worried about the most vulnerable and fragile of the Kwan children, the three-week-old infant girl who had been taken during the raid on their home. She had no idea what had happened to the baby, the rest of her family, or anything in the world beyond the garbage dump.

~

Unbeknownst to Betty, by late 1967 and early 1968, her own Guangdong Province had become the raging epicenter of some of the worst violence of the Cultural Revolution. Raids on the houses of intellectuals, teachers, professionals, artists, and journalists—or anyone with a claim to more knowledge or property than a "peasant worker"—were intense. Mao turned his own people against each other: pupil against professor, worker against employer, son against father, neighbor against neighbor. In a society built on ancestral traditions of respect for one's elders, this tore at the very fabric of moral life. One survivor later wrote, "... the moral foundation of Chinese civilization was shattered to its roots."[4]

In both Guangxi and Guangdong Provinces, there are many reports of both soldiers and civilians committing cannibalism.[5] There are now numerous, documented eyewitness accounts and confessions; many are recorded in excruciating detail, and some were confessed to without any apparent shame. Among the documented cases of cannibalization are the 421 people who were cannibalized in Guangxi. It is estimated that many thousands participated. Many of these accounts refer to the organs and flesh of dismembered enemies being consumed in communal banquets.[6]

4 Paul T.P. Wong, *Autobiography: A Lifelong Search for Meaning: Lessons on Virtue, Grit, and Faith*, March 20, 2017. http://www.drpaulwong.com/hong-kong-a-haven-for-chinese-refugees/.
5 Song Yongyi, "What is the Chinese Cultural Revolution?" CSUSB Modern China Lecture Series (Los Angeles, CA, 2017); Yi Zheng, *Scarlet Memorial: Tales of Cannibalism in Modern China* (Boulder, CO: Westview Press, 1996), 22.
6 Zheng, *Scarlet Memorial*, 110–111; VanderKlippe; Song Yongyi, "Chronology of Mass Killings during the Chinese Cultural Revolution (1966–1976)," Online Encyclopedia of Mass Violence, August 25, 2011.

Supplemental Information

Documentation on the Cultural Revolution

Until the past decade, there has been a dearth of documentation on the Chinese Cultural Revolution, which resulted in the deaths of millions and scarred an entire populace. Betty had little way of knowing that what she suffered was part of a playbook, a series of tortures used again and again by the Red Guard and PLA. Because the regime responsible for the Cultural Revolution is still in power, it has not been safe for people within China to write about the atrocities.

But some official documents have now been declassified, and many other documents and personal stories have slowly been gathered by patient researchers, some of whom smuggled official documents out of the country at great risk.

Brave scholars like historian Song Yongyi have ensured that the history of the Cultural Revolution is preserved.[7] Though a legal American resident, he was imprisoned in China for 100 days in 1999 while gathering documents on a research trip for his archives. Song was accused by the Chinese government of smuggling secret documents. Once released and returned to America, he kept up his quest and became the repository for many smuggled documents, which he has compiled and published. Among other documents, he obtained a thirty-six volume secret government report on the Cultural Revolution in the country's southern Guangxi Province, which borders Guangdong.[8]

The reports collected by Song, Tan Hecheng, and others detail many brutal forms of killing, including live burial, beating, stabbing, drowning, explosion, hanging, burning, and being driven off cliffs.[9]

---

7   Verna Yu, "'Enemy of the people' historian Song Yongyi gives as good as he gets," *South China Morning Post*, February 19, 2013: https://www.scmp.com/news/china/article/1153447/enemy-people-historian-song-yongyi-gives-good-he-gets.

8   Nathan VanderKlippe, "Suppressed records revealed 50 years after China's Cultural Revolution," *The Globe and Mail*, May 15, 2016 (updated 2018): https://www.theglobeandmail.com/news/world/suppressed-records-revealed-50-years-after-chinas-cultural-revolution/article30028854/.

9   Tan Hecheng, *The Killing Wind: A Chinese County's Descent into Madness During the Cultural Revolution*, translated by Stacy Mosher and Guo Jian (New York: Oxford University Press, 2017), 21.

They speak of more cruelty in inner Mongolia, of tongues and eyes cut out. Elsewhere and more common was branding on human flesh, immolation, mass drownings, and forcing "enemies of the people" to eat excrement and drink urine.[10] A generation of children like Betty became political orphans. Some of the most unthinkable atrocities are now documented in scrupulous detail.

Records from Song's collection also report cannibalism: "Whipped into a fury by the chaos of the times, Red Guards— groups of youth dedicated to removing enemies through violent class struggle—feasted on the [body parts] of people deemed class enemies." In total, 421 people were eaten in at least thirty-one provincial counties, according to documents obtained by Song. Cannibalism is also documented within Guangdong Province, the home of the Kwans. The perpetrators were not punished.[11]

---

10 Dikotter, *The Cultural Revolution*, 190; Zheng, *Scarlet Memorial*, 116. Zheng estimates that 10,000 to 20,000 people engaged in cannibalism in Wuxuan County alone.

11 VanderKlippe, "Suppressed records revealed"; Zheng, *Scarlet Memorial*, 22, 116.

Chapter 5

The Nadir

"Sometimes one has suffered enough to have the right to never say:
I am too happy."

– Alexandre Dumas, *The Black Tulip*

It was eight or nine months into the first year of Betty's ordeal in the garbage dump when she was dragged to the gravel in the village center, where people used to meet, talk, and play music together. In the town square that day, she saw her mother, grandmother, brother Kim, his wife, brothers Michael and King, and sister Kathy. Betty also saw Kim's mother-in-law, who had come before the raid to be with her daughter during her new pregnancy. They were kneeling in a line. All of them had been gathered, her grandmother and her mother from jail and her siblings from the labor camps where they had been scattered.

With dread, Betty saw Kim and his wife set apart. Kim and his wife had been married for only a short time, and she was newly pregnant when the raid on the Kwan home occurred. Now she was heavily pregnant. In Chinese patriarchal culture, the eldest son has an important role carrying on the lineage, the name, and the honor of the family. Kim, deeply valued by both parents, had fulfilled expectations by running many of the family businesses, then marrying and producing an heir with his wife. Now, two mothers watched their children become the malevolent focus of the guards' attention.

Once again, the villagers had been gathered into a large horde and incited by soldiers and social pressure to verbally and physically attack the family. Since these "enemies of the people" were not viewed as human, the community's rage, frustration, fear, jealousy, and hatred could be projected onto them with no apparent reservation or shame.

The family was pushed together and made to kneel in a line with their eyes to the ground. The roar of the crowd was overwhelming; they called them devils. The kneeling quickly became tiring. Grandmother Kwan was kneeling to Betty's left, her tiny bound feet visible to Betty and achingly familiar. Betty's younger sister Wendy was absent, still harbored in a safe house by a family friend.

Betty's brother King was on her right, and her mother one down from King. It became clear that her eldest brother Kim and his wife were central to the drama for which they had all been gathered. The guards' long guns were pointed at the whole family until the last moment, when they swung to the young couple. Suddenly the crowd was silenced, and Betty heard her brother call out, "Mother, what have I done wrong?" Then his wife exclaimed, "I am afraid! I don't want to die!" Then came the explosive sound of shots. Betty peeked up and saw her brother Kim slumped over to the side, his wife beside him. Both were bloodied, dead from rifle shots to the back.[1]

The bodies of Kim and his wife remained on the ground, and the soldiers dispersed the crowd and brought the family forward underneath the oak tree in the center of the meeting area. The guards mocked Tak-chui by yelling, "Why doesn't your God help you now?" They pinned her face-down on the ground, a guard standing on each arm and leg. Her own children were forced to throw small rocks at her, spit at her, and kick her. Their legs were unbound to free them to kick. Although Betty could not bring herself to do it, she was glad that her mother was facedown and could not see them. The guards were laughing and laughing, saying, "Do more! Do more!" Her mom became silent, perhaps unconscious.

---

1 The PLA commonly used a Type 56 assault rifle, which had a permanently attached stiletto-style bayonet under the barrel. It is a feature common to many Chinese-made AK-47s as well. This is likely the weapon with which Betty became so familiar.

The guards took a metal bar from the yoke of a water buffalo used in the rice fields and heated it in a fire. When the bar was glowing hot, the guards pressed it into her mother's back, first vertically the whole length of her back, and then horizontally across both shoulder blades. Betty smelled the burning cloth first, and then the burning flesh. She saw the hot metal searing the flesh black, and then at one point on the lower back, break through to white bone. The bar was held on her mom's flesh until the burns were so deep, the scars would be permanent. They had branded her with a cross.

Before the guards took the family members back to their imprisonment, they gathered their thumbprints on a strip of paper, presumably to prove their presence at the execution of the eldest Kwan son. The paper was placed on the ground and each person's right thumb inked red. When it was Betty's turn, she could not press on the paper well enough to get a distinct print. A guard stepped on her thumb with his boot and ground it, tearing it so it bled and white bone was visible.[2]

~

Roughly a year into Betty's ordeal, several months after the execution of Kim and his wife, the guards brought her baby sister to her. The little girl had been a three-week-old newborn at the time the family was crushed and scattered. Until the traditional naming ceremony at one month, where the grandmother chooses a name, a child is known by their number. This baby was Ten. The naming event is celebrated with a party, attended by family and friends. Baby number Ten had never had her party, and thus had never been named. Betty did not know for sure what happened to her in the months between the raid and being brought to the garbage dump—perhaps the baby's nanny cared for her. In any case, when baby Ten was around a year old, she too was turned out on the dump with her older sister, the Devil Child.

The guards laid the baby on Betty's lap. She was remarkably beautiful. The guards released Betty's bound hands so she could hold

---

2 Betty's thumb and nail became scarred, her thumbnail thick and uneven, one of the many permanent marks of the Cultural Revolution.

her sister. The baby wanted to crawl and toddle around, but in the filth of the garbage dump there was nowhere for her to go. There was no clean water for her to drink or with which to bathe her. It was difficult and dangerous to sneak to the dirty creek water.

At night, the guards would occasionally be absent or a guard would pretend not to see so Betty could get creek water for the baby. She warmed water in her mouth to give to her. When Betty cried, baby Ten would lick her tears. Betty was resolute; she would save her sister. When water was not available, she gave the baby her own saliva, until that too dried up. She tried to feed her with the scraps and an occasional live snake or insect when she could find and catch one. She pre-chewed whatever nourishment she could find to make it more palatable. Sometimes she had to feed the baby dirt and leaves.

Betty was desperate to save her baby sister. She wanted there to be life and smiles and baby talk in the garbage dump. After a silent year, she was finally having a face-to-face relationship of mutually shared smiles and eye contact. She gave the effort every ounce of her will.

After about two months, baby Ten seemed heavier to carry and would not eat. Betty noticed the baby would no longer smile and babble at her. She saw that while the baby's eyes were still open, they were covered with a white film and her stomach had become tightly bloated. Finally, she noticed that her baby sister had begun to emit a horrible stench.

Deciding to take a huge calculated risk, she stood up with the baby and hobbled out of the dump area toward the village. When the guard did not stop her, she knew that something must be terribly wrong. No one stopped her as she made her slow and painful way to the home of her relative. She remembers how difficult it was to walk with her ankles chained, and how heavy the baby was to carry. It took her a long time.

When she knocked on the door, it was opened by her kin shouting, "Go away! You are a Devil Child." Betty wanted to ask them for help, but when she tried to speak, she realized that she had become mute. Another relative came out on the step and pushed her down, then kicked her. As she began to fall, she switched the baby to her right arm to keep the baby's head from hitting the ground. Betty landed on her left shoulder, injuring it badly. Though the baby was beyond help, Betty still felt compelled to try to protect her. It was not until a young man whispered to Betty on her way back to the dump, "That child is dead," that she knew for sure. The baby was gone. Betty later found out the man was imprisoned for that brief kindness.

The Red Guard had placed the baby there with Betty to die a slow death, knowing that without food, water, or shelter, her survivability in the garbage dump would be measured in weeks or at most months. Regardless, Betty felt that she had failed. Intense guilt and anguish overwhelmed her. The daily taunts of "Devil Child," the complete isolation from her community, and the rejection by extended family made her question whether the heckling was true. The warm emotional shelter of her former life had become a dream. The solid attachment that had formed her early sense of self was fading. Maybe she was a Devil Child, and maybe she deserved this suffering. After all, she had not been able to save her baby sister.

The summer pajamas Betty wore had wide legs. She managed to tear off the bottoms at the knee in order to have some cloth in which to wrap baby Ten for burial. Digging a rough hole with her hands, she buried her little sister as best she could beyond the edge of the dump. Several days later, a few members of the Red Guard gloated to her that the feral dogs had unearthed and eaten her sister's body. From time to time, the guards taunted her, telling her that her brothers had died in the labor camp. She had no way of knowing whether or not this was true.

~

The young girl who was barely surviving the extremes of misery in a garbage dump miraculously continued to endure, one day at a time. But things grew worse. Sometime in Betty's second year in the garbage dump, she was again harshly hauled to the village square. This place had become a macabre scene of degeneracy. Betty could hear the laughing and yelling crowd before she saw them. Her stomach tightened and her heart roared; she knew that such a summoning could only mean horror.

When Betty arrived, the first thing she saw was her mom tied to a tall stake in the ground, her arms pulled tightly above her and bound with rope. Her mother's belly was distended with a pregnancy of perhaps six or seven months. It did not occur to Betty's innocent mind that her mother had been raped in prison.

The other incarcerated siblings had also been gathered, as before, and forced to the front of the yelling crowd. The guards placed the Kwan children on their knees close to their mother, the better to observe the scene. The guards took turns beating Betty's mother with belts and ropes, over and over, especially around her midsection. Suddenly, Betty saw a tiny baby boy drop from her mother's body, followed by the afterbirth. The soldiers were upon the infant immediately, beating him to death. Then the baby was cannibalized.

Of all the things that Betty had experienced in this dark world, this was the most abhorrent, the most dehumanizing. Seeing her own mother in such pain and humiliation and witnessing this depravity was almost more than her psyche could bear.

When Betty was returned to the garbage dump, she was afraid that she would somehow contaminate others because of what she had seen. Trauma embedded itself into her body's memory.

Supplemental Information

Good and Evil

Survivors of similar evils give valuable perspective. Aleksandr Solzhenitsyn survived imprisonment and torture in Soviet gulags for eight years after he criticized Josef Stalin in a private letter. He wrote these famous words, "If only it were all so simple! If only there were evil people somewhere insidiously committing evil deeds, and it were necessary only to separate them from the rest of us and destroy them. But the line dividing good and evil cuts through the heart of every human being. And who is willing to destroy a piece of his own heart?" [3] *The capacity of the human heart for evil is matched by its capacity for goodness and beauty.*

During the Cultural Revolution, some people risked everything to save lives. Others surrendered themselves to the absolute depths of sadism. The problem of human evil is epitomized by what Betty experienced. How could it be that so many ordinary people gave themselves over to such inhumanity? It is tempting to say they must have been inherently flawed, perhaps biologically or psychologically deficient, but the sheer number of people who participated in the darkness of the Cultural Revolution confirms that even "regular" people, under certain circumstances, participate in immoral atrocities.

Sadly, the Cultural Revolution is not unique. In recent history, even since the horrors of the Holocaust in World War II, there have been repeated genocides. The Khmer Rouge killed 1.7 million people in Cambodia between 1975 and 1979. The Bosnian genocide ripped apart the former Yugoslavia in 1992. The Rwandan massacre claimed half a million lives, mostly ethnic-minority Tutsis, in 1994.

Philip Zimbardo, an expert on everyday evil, notes the common confluence of circumstances leading to the change from humanity to inhumanity. It includes a persistent dehumanization of the victim, as in Mao's five Black Categories that labeled certain people as "other"

---

3 Aleksandr Solzhenitsyn, *The Gulag Archipelago 1918–1956* (New York: HarperCollins, 2007). 168.

and unworthy. This is followed by a deindividuation of the self, and an immersing of personal identity in a larger collective, which then diffuses personal responsibility. The Red Guard and PLA became so identified with their powerful role and group membership that they stopped thinking of themselves as former neighbors and friends and gave themselves over to the tidal wave of violence for which they did not take personal responsibility.

Next comes blind obedience to authority and an uncritical conformity with the group. The suspension or blunting of conscience in the service of a group mentality was necessary for the cruelty that occurred. Mao incited them from the top, and their cadre leaders reinforced the instructions to beat, pilfer, humiliate, and kill. Few chose to disobey.

And finally, there must be passive tolerance for evil, either through inaction or indifference.[4] Many who were not directly under attack chose to look away rather than engage and endanger themselves.

Rather than take false comfort in thinking that such a circumstance could not happen here or now, we do well to remember George Santayana's warning: "Those who do not learn history are doomed to repeat it."[5]

---

4 Philip Zimbardo, "The psychology of evil," TED Talks, 2008: https://www.ted.com/talks/philip_zimbardo_the_psychology_of_evil; Philip Zimbardo, The Lucifer Effect: Understanding How Good People Turn Evil (New York: Random House, 2007).

5 Nicholas Clairmont, "'Those Who Do Not Learn History Are Doomed To Repeat It.' Really?" *Big Think*, September 7, 2020: https://bigthink.com/culture-religion/those-who-do-not-learn-history-doomed-to-repeat-it-really/

Chapter 6

The Long Ordeal Continues

"… suffering produces endurance, and endurance produces character, and character produces hope, and hope does not put us to shame because God's love has been poured into our hearts…"

– Romans 5:3-5 (ESV)

What happened to Betty's family occurred in the context of massive cultural disruption. No one went untouched. The destruction reached all elements of culture, including religion, art, and scholarship. During the ten years of the Cultural Revolution, "goodness and beauty went underground [and] ugliness and evil were given wanton release."[1] The elders were taunted and humiliated by the youth. The laborer skilled in agriculture was sent to lead an office, while the educated professional was sent to the countryside to be "reformed by labor." The physician tried to learn to plant rice while the farmer was reeducated as a "barefoot doctor."[2] Families disintegrated. Food production declined, and by the time Chairman Mao died on September 9, 1976, 20 percent of the population (200 million people) suffered from chronic malnutrition.[3]

1 Feng Jicai, *Ten Years of Madness: Oral Histories of China's Cultural Revolution* (San Francisco: China Books and Periodicals, 1996), v.
2 Dikotter, *The Cultural Revolution*, 267–269.
3 Ibid., 263–266, 271.

Commerce was shut down and China went silent to the outside world. Many schools were closed, especially high schools and universities, resulting in a generation of Chinese youth who lost their opportunity to pursue an education. For years, universities did not give exams. By 1978, 30 to 40 percent of all children were illiterate or semi-literate. In some parts of the country, the rate reached more than 50 percent.[4]

In Mao's attempt to cleanse China of bourgeois elements (and thus eliminate anyone he saw as a threat to his power), he took aim at intellectuals, professionals, business owners, landowners, and masters of literature and the arts.[5] In 1964, Mao condemned gardening and gardeners as bourgeois because he said they were created by and for the "exploiting classes."[6] Grass and flowers were torn up. People laid waste to parks and flowers, trees, and bushes, as beauty fell into dying heaps.[7]

The words and slogans of the Cultural Revolution, which had the power to ruin lives, became numbing in their repetition. They were words like "counter-revolutionary," "capital roadist," "rightist," "bourgeois," "ox ghost" and "snake demon," "white expert," "black gang," "bad element," "bad background," and "enemy of the party."[8] Or, in Betty's case, "Devil Child." These labels were so far-reaching, and their interpretation so broad, that anybody could be accused. Each person believed they could be next, contributing to the mass hysteria. The nonsensical nature of this time is captured in a quote from Jiang Qing, Mao's wife and party leader: "If good people beat bad people, it serves them right; if bad people beat good people, the good people achieve glory; if good people beat good people, it is a misunderstanding; without beatings you do not get acquainted and then no longer need to beat them."[9]

Chairman Mao and his Cultural Revolution Group used fear, programmed mass hysteria, and total control to unleash depravity that

4 Ibid., 288.
5 Ibid., 38–41; Jicai, *Ten Years of Madness*, 43, 63–65.
6 Michael Schoenhals, *China's Cultural Revolution, 1966-1969: Not a Dinner Party* (M.E. Sharpe Incorporated, 1996); Wang Youqin, *Victims of the Cultural Revolution: An Investigative Account of Persecution, Imprisonment and Murder* (Hong Kong: Kaifang Magazine Press, 2004).
7 Dikotter, *The Cultural Revolution*, 86, 257.
8 Spence, *Mao Zedong*,164–165.
9 Dikotter, *The Cultural Revolution*, 74.

quickly unraveled morality, loyalty, and common sense. The outcome was brokenness and ashes; a 5,000-year-old civilization, which had produced some of the most advanced, subtle, and sublime human achievements, was robbed of its history and culture. Millions of homes, schools, temples, churches, libraries, and museums were denuded of their treasures. Art, including calligraphy, architecture, literature, sculptures, and paintings, was destroyed. Because artists and teachers were often the target of revolutionary zeal, China also lost many of those people who so beautifully wielded the pen, the brush, and the intellect.[10] Millions of yuan worth of treasures, musical instruments, precious porcelain, books, scrolls, jewelry, and gold were stolen. Some was taken by the Red Guard for themselves, while a larger amount was meticulously cataloged and warehoused, later to be stolen by Mao's Cultural Revolution Group, the elder statesmen of the revolution. What was not stolen was left to rot in storage.[11]

Following day after day of carnage at the hands of the Red Guard and, later, the People's Liberation Army, an ancient culture lost many of its riches. In Tibet alone, thousands of temples were destroyed. One of the irreplaceable casualties of this rampage was the home of Confucius in Shandong Province. The revered scholar and sage, whose philosophy permeated Chinese culture, was seen as a threat to Mao's power. Confucian philosophy insisted that a ruler must care for his people. Mao himself said, "Confucius is humanism, that is to say, People-centered-ism,"[12] and thus antithetical to Mao's control and rule.

In regards to the human toll, some estimate that ten million people were persecuted.[13] Others say it was ten times that. Worse yet was the loss of human life. Mao preached, "The more people you kill the more revolutionary you are."[14] Sources vary in their estimates of the death

---

10 Ibid., 38, 40–41.
11 Ibid., 89, 90.
12 Jon Halliday and Jung Chang. *Mao: The Unknown Story* (United Kingdom: Knopf, 2005), 522.
13 Aristide R. Zolbert, Astri Suhrke, and Sergio Aguayo, *Escape from Violence: Conflict and the Refugee Crisis in the Developing World* (United Kingdom: Oxford University Press, 1989).
14 Editors. "The Cultural Revolution, 50 Years On. It Was the Worst of Times," *The Economist*, May 14, 2016: https://www.economist.com/china/2016/05/14/it-was-the-worst-of-times.

toll, ranging from 500,000 to eight million. Song Yongyi, the archivist and publisher for much of the smuggled material on the Cultural Revolution, estimates about three million were killed.[15]

The teenagers of the Red Guard were manipulated into and praised for violence; they were commissioned to destroy the fabric of Chinese family life, tradition, and culture. They marauded against their teachers and parents, their friends and neighbors. Mao called on "youth radicals" to "bombard the headquarters." This gave them the encouragement they needed to attack all elders, including teachers, parents, and party officials."[16]

The PLA was told to support the destructive activity of the Red Guard. They tied up teachers and other formerly respected elders, hands painfully extended behind them in the "jet plane" position. Soldiers cut women's long hair. Many were made to don dunce hats and, like Betty, wear wooden signs with their "crime" written or their names crossed out in red, as was done for prisoners about to be executed. They were beaten, often to death, or tortured until they died by suicide.[17] They were made to bow for hours while being "struggled against."

They were sometimes, like the children of the garbage dump, forced to eat human waste, drink urine, or eat other things such as nails, ink, hair, and stones.[18] Some were made to kneel on broken glass. Families were tied together and thrown into the rivers to drown.[19] They were whipped with brass buckles from the Red Guard's belts and kicked until unrecognizable.[20] Song Yongyi writes of the darkness of that decade: "There is no clear boundary between human beings and animals. If you subvert normal social order, people could very easily cross that

---

15 Song, "What is the Chinese Cultural Revolution?"; Song, "Chronology of Mass Killings."

16 Cheek, *Mao Zedong and China's Revolutions*, 26–27.

17 Wen, *The Red Mirror*, 160; Dikotter, *The Cultural Revolution*, see pictures 210ff; Chen Ruoxi, *The Execution of Mayor Yin* (Bloomington: Indiana University Press, 2004), xiv, 11, 31; Tan, *The Killing Wind*, 21, 113–118; Jicai, *Voices from the Whirlwind*, 9, 21, 25, 56.

18 Wang, *Victims of the Cultural Revolution*.

19 Tan, *The Killing Wind*, 21.

20 Dikotter, *The Cultural Revolution*, 60–63,75; Wen, *The Red Mirror*, 13, 160; Jicai, *Voices from the Whirlwind*, viii, 26, 31, 35, 85; Tan, *The Killing Wind*, 117. Ruoxi, *The Execution of Mayor Yin*, xiv, 11, 31.

boundary from human beings to animals."[21] As horrific as Betty's suffering was, and that of her mother and siblings, it was common fare in the Cultural Revolution.

~

Betty's home boasted a beautiful coffee table photo book of Kaiping, which included a picture of the steepled, white church her grandfather helped build on the family compound.[22] Directly behind it was the blind girls' house and the lepers' house. In the church courtyard, with its expansive green lawn, was a large, red-roofed, rectangular well with a cupola top. A wooden bucket sealed at the seams with a light-colored material usually sat on the rim. This bucolic setting was the next site of Betty's torment.

The PLA and Red Guard who monitored Betty and the other imprisoned children of the garbage dump grew bored. They made the children sit cross-legged on the grass and commanded them not to move. When Betty ultimately did, she was taken from the garbage dump to the church courtyard on her own family compound and squeezed into the bucket by the well, face-down. The guards let the rope down until Betty's nose and mouth were submerged in the well water. When she was nearly drowning, they would draw her up a few inches, before submerging her again.

When they tired of this game, they would tie off the rope and leave her dangling in the well. At the worst of times she would spend a full day and night this way. The well was scary at night because it echoed, especially when a frog would leap into the water.

However, when she was in the well, she was able to quench her thirst with clean and sweet water, a respite from drinking the dirty, muddy stream water that ran through the garbage dump and the soldiers' urine. She could also catch water beetles to eat, and sometimes frogs and leaves. She would catch the frogs, scratching at their belly, tearing and peeling off the skin, so she could eat them in one bite.

---

21 Song, "What is the Chinese Cultural Revolution?"
22 Schukwing, *Kaiping Diaolou*, 2002, 92.

Another form of punishment and sadistic entertainment that Betty endured was being taken to the local cemetery and placed in a wooden coffin that had recently been exhumed. A partially decomposed corpse was still inside. She was made to spend the whole night lying beside the decaying corpse, which was full of fat, white maggots. Betty's tormentors also forced her to eat the maggots, while they laughed and mocked her.[23]

Other torments included digging a child-sized hole, forcing Betty into it, and covering her with dirt, burying her alive to the point of near suffocation.[24] They forced Betty to chew on rocks, eventually breaking all but six of her teeth to the gumline, making chewing painful and the mastication of insects and frogs almost intolerable. They pulled out Betty's toenails with pliers. They plucked out her eyebrows.

Another common torture was for the guards to place the children's hands on hot rocks until they seared through and the skin blistered. They also made frequent threats to tie each of Betty's legs to separate water buffaloes and herd each animal in a different direction, ripping her body apart.

This very young girl's chronic mental and physical agony knew no bounds. Betty's torture exceeded that of the other prisoners; even among her fellow victims, the Devil Child stood out. The sign she wore around her neck made her a target, but it also protected her. While they threatened, abused, and despised her, they were cautious about killing her outright. This was the paradoxical effect of the fearful power attributed to the Devil Child.

~

---

23 Because of the traditional Chinese respect and deference paid to the dead, and the high value on filial piety and care for one's ancestors, torments involving the dead were particularly shocking. In this area of China, bodies were buried in coffins for a period of around five years, after which the caskets were dug up and the bones removed and ritually cleaned, and then placed into an urn. The jewelry and coins buried with the body were recovered and were thought to possess spiritual or magical power. According to traditional beliefs, by desecrating a dead body the Red Guard risked unloosing a "hungry ghost."

24 Later reports document that live burial was a common form of killing during this time (Tan, *The Killing Wind*, 466).

One day, the Red Guard came to Betty with what they said was a message from her Grandmother Ng. Her mother's mother had come from America before the Cultural Revolution to visit her Kaiping hometown in order to help her daughter. Word of the political unrest had come to California, and Grandmother Ng was worried about her daughter and grandchildren. While in Kaiping, she stayed with an extended family member in her home village. Betty had stayed with Grandmother Ng in that home before the raid, so she knew where the house was. The guards said that her grandmother was asking for her and wanted to take care of her and her imprisoned mother. The Red Guard offered to take Betty to her grandmother but said they needed her to show them the way. They were convincing.

This message filled Betty with hope. Perhaps her ordeal in the garbage dump was over. Perhaps, like her sister Wendy, she was to be rescued. Perhaps her being a Devil Child had not kept her grandmother from caring about her. So she set out with the Red Guard, walking with them many miles to the house where her Grandmother Ng was staying.

Betty entered the home first, full of anxious anticipation and hope. What she saw crushed her. Her grandmother had hanged herself. She was dressed in her finery, with beautiful shoes, knowing she was about to enter the next world and determined to be well-dressed for the occasion. She hung less than a foot above the ground from a noose she had apparently fashioned herself. Her face was mottled a strange color. Someone had warned her that the Red Guard had found out her location and were on their way. Rather than face imprisonment, she released herself from this life.

The guards who had tricked Betty into revealing her grandmother's location now cut Grandmother Ng down. They took the body outside to an animal pen and put the corpse on the ground. Then they made Betty lie down all through the night by her grandmother's body. They mocked her and laughed, telling her that she had killed her grandmother.

Betty felt enormous shame and guilt about having been deceived into revealing her grandmother's location. She was returned to the garbage dump, certain now that any hope was itself a trick.

~

One of the longest lasting and mortifying repercussions of Betty's imprisonment was the loss of education. In the Kwan family, the education of both boys and girls was paramount. Betty's older siblings had received excellent education in boarding school and at a prestigious university in Hong Kong. Those not yet sent to boarding school were educated at home. Betty, at seven, had already received training from her grandmother in intricate embroidery and sewing, and was eagerly absorbing what she could over the shoulders of her older siblings. But her formal education had not yet begun when the Cultural Revolution undid her home.

She was a bright, inquisitive child with a nimble and quick mind. She longed to learn. One day, she took a risk and crept away from the garbage dump to the nearby school building where young children were being taught. She stood underneath the window, trying to hear what the teacher was saying. The principal saw her and alerted the Red Guard. The guards brought out a box of broken glass and shoved her into it on her bare knees, a common Red Guard tactic, while the schoolchildren walked by her in single file and spat on her.[25] The guards made her stay on the glass for hours, drawing deep cuts on both knees. They threw salt water on her cuts to make them sting. If the cuts stopped bleeding, she was jostled purposely so they would break open and bleed again. It was a long and excruciating healing process, and the scars were a constant reminder that education was not permitted for her.

---

25 Dikotter, *The Cultural Revolution*, 63.

Chapter 7

The Escape

"Courage is rightly esteemed the first of human qualities because...
it is the quality which guarantees all others."
– Winston Churchill, *Great Contemporaries*

"Injustice in the end produces independence."
– Voltaire

One night, Betty, now ending her tenth year, was lying at her spot on the dump when she felt a presence behind her. A hand covered her mouth. She heard her older sister Kathy whisper urgently, "We are going." Betty had not seen Kathy since the day their mother had been beaten to miscarriage.

The risk of awakening the nearby guard was enormous. Betty was confused and scared, and wanted to ask where they were going, but by that time, she was no longer capable of speaking.

Kathy lifted Betty quietly to her feet, and saw that her legs were shackled at the ankle in an iron chain. Fearful of making noise that would alert the guards, Kathy hoisted Betty over her shoulder, holding Betty's feet together with one hand. The chain still clanked loudly and threatened to give them away, and they had to stop and hide a short distance from the dump, delaying their escape. Finally, they were able to pound off the chain so that at least one foot was free and Betty could walk. Eventually, another traveler on the road, a man known to Kathy, cut the ankle chain off and threw it into the river. For the first time in a long time, Betty felt free; the weight was off her feet.

Kathy had already been to the camps where their brothers Michael and King were held and had managed to get them out before helping Betty. Her initial intention was to rescue and escape only with her brothers, because she knew it was unlikely the boys would be allowed to live. She had witnessed their brother Kim being executed, and knew Michael and King could well be next. Because Chinese culture sees the sons as the vehicle of the family lineage, Kathy felt compelled by honor and duty to save the family tree. Kathy was more ambivalent about the risk of rescuing Betty, especially because she was not entirely certain that Betty's "Devil Child" reputation was not true. However, the route Kathy and the boys were traveling as they fled took them near the garbage dump, and Kathy decided to try to get Betty as well. Kathy, ten years older than Betty, was roughly seventeen when the Cultural Revolution destroyed her family and twenty when she managed to gather her three starving and traumatized younger siblings from imprisonment.

Kathy's rescue attempt was audacious, dangerous, and almost certainly doomed to fail. After she collected Betty from the garbage dump and managed to get her chain off, the children went to where their paternal grandmother, Grandmother Kwan, now was in hiding after being released from prison. They told her they were making a run for it in hopes of swimming across Deep Bay and finding their father in Hong Kong. Grandmother gave them eight gold coins, held together with a cord through a hole in each coin. She told them that if any of the siblings died along the way or drowned during the swim, the others should tie a coin to them. This would ensure their "passport to heaven."[1]

The young Kwan siblings had no maps or any kind of navigational equipment. Without a compass or map, they were destined to wander with only a vague idea of their direction. They had no shoes, no clothes but the rags they wore, and no food. They had no money and would not part with grandmother's gold coins. More dangerous, they had no

---

[1] Betty still has those coins, which were on display in the California Museum for Women, History and the Arts in Sacramento as part of the Minerva Award exhibition.

These coins were to act as a "passport to heaven" for the children should they die in their escape effort.

travel documents, which ensured that the heavily patrolled roads and trails would likely result in their capture.

They began their journey in late winter, just after the Chinese New Year. Even in a subtropical climate, at that time of year the weather was cold and frigid, with winter monsoons blowing from the north. There was snow on the coast that particular year.

They followed others trying to make their way to Deep Bay and across it to Hong Kong. Most of the travelers were as uninformed and desperate as Betty and her siblings. They would join up with one group, then another. Sometimes they would wander in circles in the same area for weeks at a time. They could only walk at night, and never on a night with a full moon. Betty had adapted acute night vision by this time. They had to wait for the farmers and others to go to bed before they continued their journey, and then hide themselves safely away before the people arose again. The populace in general was so frightened of punishment from the Red Guard and PLA that they would turn in escapees if they found them.

During the day, the children climbed and hid in the tea trees with broad leaves, or in the reeds and rushes and rice fields. The fields were wet and muddy, but they provided leeches to eat. The siblings lived like this, on the run, without resources, not knowing where they were going from one season to the next. They ate dead snakes they found on the road, as well as bugs and leaves. Sometimes they were able to get food from the pockets of the dead strewn along the paths and roads: people who had been shot by PLA soldiers or died of disease or exposure. The corpses of escapees were everywhere. Occasionally, they found dried rice or dried meat on a body. Because of Betty's broken teeth, chewing was difficult. Wide, green leaves were best.

While the journey from Kaiping to Hong Kong is not far by boat, the children had to go on land. They were forced to take a long, circuitous route: north around the Pearl River Delta, and then east and south to reach the narrow Deep Bay where they could finally swim across to Hong Kong. Considering the daily miles and number of months of travel, the children covered well over a thousand miles. Travel was perilous, but at least as children, and small, malnourished, emaciated children at that, it was easier for them to hide than it was for adults. Always, night and day, they tried to keep silent. During these months, Betty was still mute, which, though frustrating, decreased the risk. She felt confused and extremely tired. Now that she was finally with her siblings again, it was upsetting for her not to be able to speak with them. Throughout the journey, the wooden sign marking Betty as a "Devil Child" hung from her neck; while the chains had been removed, the sign had become a part of her.

A particular terror on the journey were packs of large dogs, trained by the military to find and savage escapees. The dogs would roust screaming escapees out of hiding for PLA soldiers to find and shoot. As the Kwan siblings drew closer to the coast and their destination, the number of well-armed PLA increased.

One night, a dog found Betty and her siblings. All four ran as hard and fast as they could. Betty was last, and the huge yellow dog grabbed her by the buttock. The older children had climbed a tree and pulled Betty up, but the dog tore out a large chunk of her muscle and flesh. For days the children were stuck in the tree until the bleeding had slowed enough for Betty to move. They had nothing to bandage the wound, not even extra cloth to stanch it, and, of course, no medicine. They were in a hilly coastal area at the time, with steep slopes that required them to slide down on their bottoms. Every time Betty would slide, her wound would open up again. The children stopped again and again, waiting until a scab had formed over Betty's wound so they could press on.

The dog tore the pants of the pajamas Betty had been wearing since the night their home was raided more than three years ago. She had to cover up, so they took clothes from a dead man's body. They tore his pants at the knees and Betty put them on over her pajamas with a knot around her waist. This was terrifically difficult for her, deeply imbued as she was with the cultural belief that dead bodies are to be respected and not disturbed. It felt like a debt that could never be repaid.

The Kwan siblings traveled this agonizingly slow and dangerous path for about a year. After three years of horrific imprisonment, they could barely endure another year of hiding, hypervigilance, fear, and starvation. But on this journey, they were walking toward a goal, and they had each other. They fed on the strength, courage, and purpose of their togetherness. Finally, they reached a vantage point from which they could see the object of their desire: the huge expanse of the South China Sea, Deep Bay, and, in the distance, Hong Kong.

~

At last, Betty and her siblings arrived at the crossing of Deep Bay.[2] They were at the eastern edge of the Chinese mainland, near Shenzhen. In the distance, they could see Hong Kong, a dream barely hoped for, across the roughly four-mile expanse of Deep Bay.[3] It was by now likely the winter of 1970–1971, more than four years into the Cultural Revolution. The Kwan siblings could see Christmas lights shining from the Hong Kong shore, confirming that it was December or January. The four were between the ages of eleven and twenty. Betty had never before left Kaiping, but now she and her siblings had finally arrived at

---

2 Known as Hau Hoi Wan Bay in Cantonese.
3 Author Chen Bing'an said in an interview that the swim across the bay is four kilometers, or 2.4 miles (He Huifeng, "Forgotten Stories of the Great Escape to Hong Kong," *South China Morning Post*, January 13, 2013). Other sources say the refugees traveled four to six miles in the water (Ian Stewart, "Flow of Refugees to Hong Kong from Mainland China Is Rising," *The New York Times*, September 12, 1971). The disparity is likely due to variation in currents and departure and arrival points. If the children left Shenzhen and landed in Lau Fau Shan, which seems most likely, it would have been about four miles. However, based on the maps from an acount of one succssful swimmer, the Kwans may have well have taken the "West Line," which would have required about six miles of swimming (Wong, *Swimming to Freedom*, 214).

the bay that might lead them to freedom. Depending on the currents, weather conditions, and their ability to swim, it would take many hours to traverse the expanse. Of the four, only Kathy knew how to swim.

The siblings knew it was unlikely they would all have the strength to cross the water, let alone avoid being shot. It was winter again. Their tattered clothing was inadequate. Each day their starvation had grown more acute, their death nearer. They were emaciated, freezing, famished, ill, frightened, and utterly worn down. In their years of imprisonment, and then their year of escape, they had been pushed repeatedly to the brink of death. And now they were facing a long swim in frigid water with marksmen looking for them.

Soldiers of the PLA patrolled the water's edge, hunting for "criminals" who were betraying Mao's Cultural Revolution by trying to escape. Silence was key; any noise would attract the attention of the soldiers. The large dogs hunted the shore, ferreting out escapees and alerting the soldiers to their find. Soldiers arrested some of those they found, while others were wrapped in thick coils of rope and thrown into the bay to drown. The children heard voices of young men and women scream out in terror: "Please, don't drown me! Don't drown me!"

During the decade of the Cultural Revolution, from 1966 to 1976, it is estimated that as many as a million refugees made the journey to this coastline on the Shenzhen side of the Pearl River Delta.[4] Their aim was to become "Freedom Swimmers" by making it to safety on the shores of Hong Kong. Shenzhen City even had a special job description that involved helping officials collect and bury the bodies of the countless people who failed to make the crossing. Those who pulled dead bodies out of the water were called "corpse fishers" and could make fifteen yuan (about six US dollars at the time) per body.[5]

The swim was best done at night, preferably when there was little or no moon. For those who actually made it into the water, the soldiers were ready with their long rifles, doing target practice on the floating

---

4   Some sources say it was several times that, for example: Stewart, "Flow of Refugees to Hong Kong," 1971.
5   Chen Bing'an, *The Great Escape to Hong Kong* (United States: American Academic Press, 2019).

bodies. The swim was torturously long.[6] Boats patrolled the bay and the currents were strong and deadly. Sharks, attracted by the corpses, also patrolled the waters and took down many swimmers. Fatigue and cramping took down more.

The border between Hong Kong and the People's Republic of China ran through the middle of the bay; if they could get beyond the halfway point, they might survive. A beacon at the midpoint and another on the Hong Kong shore lit the way. The fishing village of Lau Fau Shan beckoned them across the treacherous expanse.[7]

The winter monsoon was blowing dry, cold air from the north. Betty wore only the remains of her tattered pajamas for the swim. Betty and her siblings crawled on their stomachs for several miles, making their slow and silent way toward the water, gripped with the fear of being scented by a dog or spied by a soldier. To have come so far only to die in the end like so many others was a possibility, even a likelihood, they had agreed to risk.

The ground was chilled so that the mud they were crawling through had stiffened overnight into small, frozen peaks. Hiding beneath the vegetation on the grimy, frosty shore, the Kwan siblings heard the cracking sounds of the PLA's victims being thrown into the frigid bay.[8] The bodies sank at first, and then surfaced and floated as they decayed, warning of the dangerous crossing the children were about to attempt.

Trembling with fear and cold, they waded into the water, slipping through the stems and roots of the salt marsh near the shore, and grabbed a branch, about five feet long and thick as a man's arm, left by escapees who hadn't made it far. They needed the branch both to hold them above the water and to screen them from the marksmen. Their emaciated bodies offered no protection from the cold. Not knowing how to properly swim, they paddled, trying to be as silent as possible.

---

6 Ian Stewart, "Chinese Refugees Swim Across a Perilous Bay to Hong Kong," *The New York Times*, June 22, 1972.

7 It might have been the village of Yuen Long, or another of the close by villages on the West Coast of Hong Kong, but Lau Fau Shan was the most frequently cited as an arrival site in this author's research (Chen, *The Great Escape to Hong Kong*).

8 While Hong Kong's climate is subtropical, intense winter monsoons can bring a cold northern air mass with sub-zero temperatures (Wong Tak-kan, "Last time it snowed in Hong Kong," *Hong Kong Observatory*). January 1971, the likely winter of Betty's crossing, was the second-to-last time snow has been recorded in Hong Kong.

They made it part of the way into the channel when their hands became numb and they lost hold of the branch. Kathy held Betty's hand; the two boys, Michael and King, held each other, and a strong eddy fortuitously threw them up on some rocks slippery with algae. They clung to the rocks and rested there for several minutes, crouching low. When Kathy saw another large branch being carried toward them by the current, she was able to grab it. This time, as the four clung to the branch, they immersed themselves completely underwater, surfacing only for breath. It was actually warmer underwater, out of the stinging wind, and they were safer from the soldiers' rifle scopes. The water tasted surprisingly salty and pleasing to their starving palates.

Suddenly the water boiled with the flash of a large fish, and they surfaced to see a shark circling them. Once again, Kathy acted quickly; she managed to strike out into the water to a dead body floating nearby. As rifle shots rang, she pulled the body by its rope bonds and sent it feet-first toward the shark, hoping to distract it. The shark swam away and the siblings, grasping their branch, submerged themselves again and paddled toward the Hong Kong shore. Kathy told the others that if another disaster struck, they were to try to make it on their own. They would all be together in heaven and it was better for someone to make it than no one.

Hour after hour, as the night waned and the sun rose, they paddled. Hypothermia set in; their limbs were numb with cold. Still they hung on, helping each other cling to the branch. As they swam farther from the Chinese shore, the rifle shots decreased and finally ceased. They were on the Hong Kong side of Deep Bay.

If they made it to the other side, Hong Kong's "touch base" policy would allow them to stay. The four had to help each other hold fast, as they had done during their long escape over land. In addition to their family bond, the four had become melded into a unit by the crisis of circumstances. The swim felt interminable. Finally, all four struggled to the shore on the Hong Kong side of Deep Bay.

As the siblings came out of the water, they were nearly at an end. The years of starvation, imprisonment, beatings, and torture had left them with only a tenuous grasp on life. Given their physical debasement, their survival seemed more a matter of will than physical possibility. Their bodies had dwindled in the four years since their home was raided, and life as they knew it had been completely destroyed. Now, against all odds, they pulled themselves out of the water and stood on safe ground.

They were stunned by all the faces peering at them and the cacophony of noises. Aid stations had been set up by Canadian, Australian, American, New Zealand, and British charities. Dozens of people crowded the shore. Confusion, fatigue, and shock competed with relief and joy. Hundreds of thousands of escapees from the Cultural Revolution had stood where the Kwan children were now standing.[9]

Betty was the second out of the water after her brother King. Kathy was the last out of the water because she had cut her knee in the crossing, and it was bleeding. The fishing village of Lau Fau Shan, where they had likely arrived, is famous for its oyster beds, and many who crossed were cut by the sharp oyster shells. Most of the swimmers were between seventeen and twenty-five, and many were escaping the forced labor camps on the mainland. Betty was a rare preteen swimmer.

When she came out of the water, Betty noticed that there was silence from the onlookers; no one did or said anything for a few moments, confused by her appearance. Her emaciated body was black with the scum of four years of filth, now marked by lighter spots where the water passage had rubbed some of the dirt away. Most startling, her hair, which should have been black, was completely white—one of the effects of chronic, severe malnutrition.[10] She wore only tattered rags. The nuns who came to help at first assumed that she was a very tiny old woman.

---

9 Exact numbers are not known. Records in Hong Kong document only officially registered refugees who presented at the immigration office. Many more simply melted into Hong Kong. Refugee organizations estimated that for every refugee officially registered, three to four more simply slipped away. This immigration office officially processed about 700,000 Chinese refugees from 1949 when Mao took power until 1974, but official numbers are likely a dramatic undercount. The Chinese government has been reluctant to declassify records from this period (Stewart, "Chinese Refugees Swim Across a Perilous Bay"). Millions of refugees fled mainland China for Hong Kong from the 1950s through the 1970s, fleeing both the famine of Mao's Great Leap Forward and the later Cultural Revolution. Between 1945 and 1970, the Hong Kong population grew from 600,000 to four million (He, "Forgotten Stories of the Great Escape").

10 Hypo-pigmentation is known to occur in those with a protein deficiency (Anagha Bangalore Kumar, Huma Shamim, and Umashankar Nagaraju, "Premature Graying of Hair," *International Journal of Trichology* 10, no. 5, 2018: 198–203).

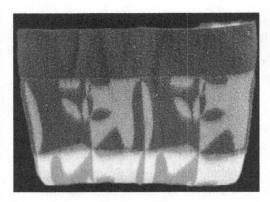

The blanket that Betty was wrapped in after crossing Deep Bay to Hong Kong

But the wooden sign that Betty had worn for four years still declared her a Devil Child in clear white lettering. A Cantonese-speaking missionary sister who seemed to belong to one of the Australian or New Zealand orders stepped forward. The nun wrapped Betty in a soft, tan and brown wool blanket and told her, "You are safe, you are safe." Then she noticed the sign around Betty's neck and read its condemnation. She looked Betty in the eyes and said gently, "You are not the devil's child. You are God's child."

Taking a pair of clippers, the sister cut the wire holding the wooden sign and pulled it from Betty's neck. The wire had grown into her skin over the years, and it was painful to have it torn out. The nun threw the sign forcefully into the water and said, "Now you are free." Betty felt naked. The words of the sign had burned into her psyche, and its familiar physical presence had come to feel like a sort of protection. She didn't think she would ever feel truly free.

Kathy gathered the siblings together. She was anxious to find their father and did not allow the children to stop to eat or drink. She did not want to register with the aid agencies, as the Kwan family name had prominence, and they were Hong Kong landholders with a father hopefully awaiting them.[11] They walked together up onto the levee. Kathy was walking slowly because of her injury, while Betty walked quickly out ahead.

---

11 If one claimed political asylum it was possible to go to Canada or America, and many made their way to North America that way. But others were afraid to claim asylum, because if they had family remaining on the Chinese mainland, those family members could be found and killed.

Five months earlier, long into their flight toward freedom, the children's father, while holding a despairing vigil in his Hong Kong home, had been told by a friend that two of his sons and two of his daughters had escaped and were trying to reach Deep Bay to attempt a crossing. These four were among the seven of his ten children who had been trapped on the mainland before he could return for them.

Betty's father had been living in his Hong Kong home those long years, consumed by remorse and shame at his miscalculation, having left his family and been unable to rescue them after they were cut off by the rapid descent of the Cultural Revolution. He had few sources of information, mostly swimmers who made it across the bay. He had no way of communicating with his family on the mainland, as China had shut out the rest of the world. Every day for the five months since he had heard of his children's escape attempt, he had come to the wooden walk above Deep Bay, where he could observe the rescue efforts. He brought a box of pastries with him as a sign of hope, which he distributed in the evening when he returned home without his children. It was incredibly unlikely the four had escaped and survived.

On the day of his children's success, he was walking the wooden planks of the levee. Betty, who had been trained by her captors for years to look down and never into a person's face, saw his familiar shoes first. She knew him. She grabbed his hand and tried to call out "Papa," but her long muted voice could not speak.

He did not recognize her or the others at first, but as he looked into their expectant faces, it became clear that, against all odds, these four wasted children were in fact his. They had survived. The moment he had almost ceased hoping for had actually arrived. They were all so changed, not only by the passage of time but also by the torture they had endured, that he could barely make out their resemblance to the children he had last seen.

Many of his friends had lost their entire family. The absolute implausibility of any of his children escaping the camps, making it to the shore to swim, and enduring those treacherous waters, let alone four of them, overwhelmed him. And when he looked at Betty, he could tell by her white hair, her scars, and her muteness that she had endured the unspeakable. He grabbed her up into his arms and hugged her tightly. Betty felt that she had finally come home. She had found a way to fly out of her prison.

Papa took his four starving children to a restaurant. Betty recalls that Michael ate twenty-three bowls of rice before their father made him stop. Then he took them to the immigration office and to receive medical care, where they were inoculated for smallpox and cholera and tested for tuberculosis. Both Michael and King were suffering from TB and were hospitalized in a special TB hospital.[12]

While the boys went off to one hospital, Betty was hospitalized in a different facility, but her father was uncomfortable with the fact that a famous opera singer had raised funds to pay for the hospitalization of Chinese refugees. He felt he had already failed his children and he was not going to compound his sense of failure by allowing someone else to pay for their medical care. He checked Betty out of the first hospital and she was admitted to a private hospital to continue her recovery.

For a long time, Betty was unable to eat normally, suffering from chronic gastrointestinal distress and diarrhea. She preferred to sleep on the floor and could not wear shoes, as her feet swelled terribly when she tried. She could not tolerate eating any kind of fresh, raw food. The memories of living on frogs, snakes, and bugs had made her averse to raw food. It took her a long time to trust that she was now safe, that she was fed, was sheltered, had plenty of fresh water to drink, and most of all, once again had her Papa. The smell of cooked food, the taste of fresh water, the comfort of a warm bath, and the smell and feel of fresh, clean clothing were all a discovery. She could hardly remember the delicious feeling of being warm and fed. As she recovered in the hospital, she slowly began to relax into being nurtured, protected, and safe once again.

Kathy, the heroic engineer of the escape, was amazingly resilient and her health quickly rebounded. She had been engaged when her life

---

12 Laurie Chen and Yujing Liu, "Explainer: how Hong Kong has for decades been a magnet for refugees and migrants," *South China Morning Post*, December 23, 2017: https://www.scmp.com/news/hong-kong/community/article/2125451/explainer-how-hong-kong-has-decades-been-magnet-refugees.

was shattered and, now free, she went almost immediately to Macau, where her fiancé's family lived, to begin the process of getting married and starting a family.[13]

While Betty recovered in the hospital, her father came to visit her daily. During one visit, she noticed that his nose was bleeding, but he seemed unconcerned. Betty's brothers King and Michael remained in the TB hospital and in recovery for a long time. Her father did not allow Betty to see her brothers and never explained it was for her own health. Though she never asked him, she feared that her father might have been trying to protect his sons from the taint of associating with Betty, the Devil Child.

Betty carried the words of the sign with her, long after it was cut from her neck.

---

13 Macau at the time was an autonomous region, having been settled and governed by the Portuguese since 1887. Although Macau sits on the South China Sea adjacent to Guangdong Province, from which the children had fled, it still had some independence during the Cultural Revolution. Kathy must have considered it safe enough to go to Macau so soon after her long imprisonment, even though by 1967 Macau had also been disrupted by the turmoil on the mainland.

Chapter 8

Life with Papa in Kowloon

"Suffering, failure, loneliness, sorrow, discouragement, and death will be part of your journey, but the Kingdom of God will conquer all these horrors. No evil can resist grace forever."

— Brennan Manning, *The Ragamuffin Gospel*

As Betty grew stronger, she was discharged from the hospital and went to live with her father in their house on the Kowloon Peninsula. Because he was a dentist, he was able to repair many of the teeth she had broken when being forced to chew on rocks.

Betty fell into a new rhythm of life in the Kowloon house, and she began to strengthen, heal, and even talk a bit. She observed that Papa's nose continued to bleed, and that he seemed thin and weak. She worried, then reassured herself that she was overreacting; Papa seemed to ignore his symptoms. But eventually he could no longer deny that something was wrong, and he agreed to go for testing. Betty went with him to the hospital for the tests and again for the results. On that second visit, the doctor, test results in hand, somberly diagnosed her father with metastatic pancreatic cancer; it was already in his liver. On the day of this diagnosis, Papa and Betty left the hospital, sat side by side on the sidewalk curb, and cried.

In Chinese culture, crying is shameful. It is not done publicly, and especially not by men. But this father and daughter, so recently reunited after a harrowing time, and so specially bonded by their family history and his yearning to protect her, were now facing the reality of a permanent separation. The dreams of family reunification and a secure future that had nurtured hope for four years were dying in the face of a terminal diagnosis. Betty's longing to be safe and protected was scorched by the fire of this new tragedy.

Betty was left to care for her father on her own during his illness. Two of Betty's aunts, whom her parents had helped to escape in the days before their home was raided, lived in the upper floors of the Kowloon house, but they did not help care for him. They believed that to have a younger sibling die before them would be bad luck and appeared to want nothing to do with the care of their younger brother. This distressed her Papa very much.

In Chinese tradition, care for the dead was normally left exclusively to the offspring. If a son died unmarried and without children, even his parents would not necessarily deal with his body or funeral. So her aunts may have felt little responsibility for their younger sibling, assuming it was Betty's job as his child. It was also common to be afraid of contamination by illness or death, bad luck caused by malign external influences, or misfortune that the sufferer may have brought upon themselves through karma. And the Kwan family had surely experienced misfortune.

Meanwhile, Michael and King remained in the TB hospital, while Kathy had moved to Macau. Betty had three much older siblings who had left the mainland before the chaos of the Cultural Revolution descended on their family: Alex, the eldest surviving son, and Faye and Pat, the eldest daughters. Faye was already living in San Francisco with her husband and children, Pat taught at a Catholic boarding school in Hong Kong and was rarely in the Kowloon House before leaving for America. Alex was at home only occasionally before he, too, left permanently for America.

For the last few years, these three elder siblings had lived a very different existence to that of the seven Kwan children trapped on the mainland. They were privileged, educated, wealthy, and cultured, and in spite of earlier hardships and political upheaval, they managed to uphold all the opportunities and expectations of that position. They could not fathom what their younger siblings had endured, and the four who had escaped were not inclined to talk about what had happened to them.

Even though the eldest surviving Kwan children did not experience the horror of the Cultural Revolution like their younger siblings, they still suffered enormous loss. Their ancestral home was crushed, their lands and property confiscated, their mother imprisoned, their eldest brother and youngest sister killed, their sister Wendy in hiding, and the family standing, businesses, and fortune mostly gone. And now their father was dying.

Betty was a tiny twelve-year-old girl with still mostly white hair who could not speak fluently due to years of enforced silence and trauma. She had trouble digesting food, could not wear shoes, was scarred deeply in body and mind, and had endured years of torture. And yet it was she who provided care for her dying father.

She fed him and helped him dress. She boiled water for him to wash his face and helped him brush his teeth. His skin turned yellow, and he gradually lost his sight. He began stumbling over small thresholds, and accused her of putting up dark curtains over the windows. She worked laboriously to get him to his treatment sessions. He was a tall man, weighing over 200 pounds before his illness, and Betty had great trouble moving him, even after he became wasted from disease. Her hands would slip trying to get him down the stairs. She would put a chair on the landing for him to sit, waiting for the taxi to take them to his chemotherapy and radiation appointments.

Papa would talk at length to Betty during their daily trips in a taxi or ferry to his treatments. He talked of his guilt for having left his wife and younger children to suffer as they did. He made Betty promise that she would take care of her younger sister Wendy, who was still on the mainland in a safe house in Guangzhou with Grandmother Kwan. Papa told Betty that if he began to sleep most of the time and stopped smoking, she should take him to the hospital.

On the day these signs manifested, although she was still able to speak only haltingly, Betty managed to call for an ambulance. She helped Papa get down the stairs to the first floor, where the medical transport workers picked him up. In the hospital, as he grew weaker, she lay on his chest, close to his heart. When he died, she covered him with the blanket the nun had given her on the shore of Deep Bay. He was fifty-one years old.

Papa's body was returned home, un-embalmed, and Betty held vigil for three days, as was the custom. She lit incense sticks stuck into bowls of rice placed at his feet to guide him to heaven. The little girl whom Papa had carried in his arms at his own father's funeral was now seeing him on his way. She went to the funeral parlor and tried to convince them, by showing them gold and paper money left by her father, that she could pay for a funeral. However, the funeral operators did not want to deal with a child, especially one as odd as Betty. In what seems emblematic of how separated the family then was, Betty did not approach her aunts for help. Instead, Betty went to her paternal uncle George's mother-in-law, an old woman living in Hong Kong. This elderly woman dealt with the funeral home on Betty's behalf.

At Papa's funeral, the old family friend Mr. Sun came to Betty with a gift of jewels and gold to pay for the casket. The last time she had seen him was when she watched him and Papa row away from her on the Kaiping dock.

Through the night of the funeral, Mr. Sun held vigil with Betty over the casket, and he told her the story of why her father had left her in Kaiping when he made his run for Hong Kong—why Betty had faced four years of torture instead of escaping to safety with Papa.

Mr. Sun had been found out and targeted by the Red Guard during a brief and ill-advised trip back to mainland China for his mother's birthday. His education, wealth, and connection to America and Harvard immediately made him an "enemy of the people." In the days before Betty's trip to the docks on Papa's back, the Red Guard descended on Mr. Sun's parental home in Kaiping and took his wife and nine children, bound, to the river. The guards forced them into huge wicker baskets used to take hogs to market. They bound the baskets with rope and threw them into the river. All nine children and his wife drowned.[1]

---

1 Drowning as a form of execution was common during the Cultural Revolution and became known as "releasing a raft" (Tan, *The Killing Wind*, 21).

Due to the strong Chinese cultural value placed on biological descendance, Betty's father may have felt obligated to help his friend escape so that he could have the chance to begin another family.[2] The fisherman also played a part when he refused to take them all. Betty was told decades later by Mr. Sun's brother, who was then living in Canada, that the fisherman knew of Betty's "Devil Child" moniker and was afraid of her.

Her father was torn by the competing needs of his vulnerable daughter in the face of danger and his dear friend who had just suffered the traumatic murder of his wife and nine children. Simply, the needs of a man without a lineage outweighed the needs of even a beloved little girl. He truly thought he would have time to come back for his family before the darkness descended on them. It was a gamble he lost. Betty paid the price.

Now, Betty had come from terror to freedom, only to lose the one person she thought might protect her. She watched her father die with a broken heart, and a part of Betty's heart died with him.

---

2 So common was the elimination of male heirs at this time in China that one author said: "Killing the offspring to eliminate a family is a great national treasure of our Chinese nation" (Zheng, *Scarlet Memorial*, 58).

Chapter 9

After the Death of Jack Kwan

"He who learns must suffer. Even in our sleep, pain that cannot forget falls drop by drop upon the heart, and in our own despair, against our will, comes wisdom to us by the awful grace of God."

– Aeschylus

This broken-hearted girl once more moved forward alone. The plan had been for Papa to accompany Betty to America where she would join her eldest sister, Faye, who was married to a Chinese American and living in San Francisco.[1] Betty had been anxious to travel with her father, to be protected by him as she began a new life, and to leave the pain of the Cultural Revolution far behind her. But once again her dreams were denied, and she had to find safe harbor within.

Her second eldest sister, Pat, had moved to Seattle with her American husband. The brothers with whom Betty escaped, Michael and King, were still recovering from TB and would have to wait another six months before gaining embassy clearance to travel to America. Their

---

1 After the death of their father, Faye had been given the task of filling out her escaped siblings' U.S. immigration and travel documents as they were preparing to immigrate to America. Because Faye had been away long before Betty was born, and all records had been lost or destroyed, she was not sure of her younger siblings' birth years, let alone birth dates. Their father was dead and their mother imprisoned. So she did her best, but could not be accurate. As a result, some of the official birth years are dramatically off. Birth dates were one of many losses in the fog of the revolution.

father had obtained an American passport for Betty, King, and Michael, which meant giving up their Hong Kong passports. Plane tickets had been purchased for Papa and Betty to fly to San Francisco on October 30.[2] He died on the day of their scheduled departure.

As a man with a medical background who had become seriously depleted over the months of his cancer treatment, Jack Kwan had to have known that he was dying and that the trip was an impossibility. But he held out hope that, as long as he was capable of clear cognition, he could escort Betty to America and absolve himself of the guilt he felt for leaving her on the dock in Kaiping all those years ago. On their frequent trips to his cancer treatments, he told Betty of the terrific sense of wrongdoing he felt about what had happened to his wife and children. His life was cut short before he was able to fully make amends—yet another in a series of tragedies that had now become familiar to a young girl whose soul was rapidly aging.

Betty stayed in Kowloon, living in the family house largely alone. Her aunts were upstairs, but they were forbidden by cultural and religious tradition from seeing Betty for 100 days after her father's death. In Chinese culture, after the death of a parent, a teen or even younger child would have been expected to take care of themselves and be independent. Basic food was provided for her to prepare, but she does not recall where it came from.

Betty thought of herself as an evil person. She had internalized the "Devil Child" sign, believing she could be contagious and that it was best she kept to herself. She felt she had no right to whine or complain because of the corruption of her very being. She could only see in herself what her tormentors had told her she was.

In the year following her father's death, it was arranged that she would fly, on her own, to meet her eldest sister in San Francisco. However, she had a task to fulfill before she could leave. While her father was dying, he made Betty promise that she would look after her younger sister Wendy. Betty had not seen Wendy since the night of the raid in 1967 when they were all separated. She knew that Wendy was

---

2 It is unclear whether this was 1971 or 1972.

still in Guangzhou, the capital city of Guangdong Province, living in a safe house with Grandmother Kwan.[3] Betty often wondered why her six-year-old sister Wendy was rescued and protected while she, only one year older, suffered in the garbage dump. One factor was her Devil Child status, which would have increased the danger to any family harboring her.

Compelled by the promise she had made to her dying father, Betty refused to leave for California until she had seen Wendy. She was determined to check on her sister before leaving for America, as she knew it would be many years before she returned, if ever.

But Betty no longer had a Hong Kong passport, and she certainly could not openly enter mainland China with her new American passport. Her sister Kathy, who had become a mother figure in her life, had come to Hong Kong to help Betty prepare for her trip to America. On the force of Betty's stubborn will, it was arranged that she would travel with Kathy to where she now lived with her husband in Macau. From there, two fishermen were hired to illegally transport Betty and Kathy ninety miles upriver to Guangzhou where Wendy and their grandmother were living. This boat was a sampan, the traditional Chinese vessel used for fishing and waterway transportation, but it was somewhat larger than the boat her father had hired when he was fleeing from Kaiping to Hong Kong years before. This larger boat could seat four to five people and was powered by two rowing fishermen.

It was a difficult and lengthy trip. They left before nightfall and traveled all night and well into the next day, an achingly long time for two sisters longing to see a third.[4] They were concerned about being found out, but the enormous activity and huge population of Guangzhou offered some protection. Once at the dock, they were transported on a three-wheeled, man-powered bicycle to the dwelling where Wendy and Grandmother Kwan lived.

Betty brought Wendy two pencils as a gift. Pencils were important

---

3 Guangzhou is also known as Canton.
4 Row boats travel at the rate of about four to five miles an hour, slightly faster with two rowers, which means this trip would have taken almost a full night and day each way (John Welsford, *Backyard Boatbuilder: How to Build Your Own Wooden Boat*, Auckland, NZ: Reed Books, 1999).

to Betty because they represented the writing she had begun to learn, and the hope that she would one day have another opportunity. She also brought a Washington Red Delicious apple to symbolize her upcoming move to America. The girls also brought an orange for their grandmother, who had no teeth with which to chew an apple.

They were in the home for what seemed like less than twenty minutes, crying at the poignancy of being in each other's presence again, when one of the fishermen whispered something in Kathy's ear. They were abruptly rushed out to the three-wheeled bicycle that took them back to the river. Apparently, their trip to the mainland had become known. They had to leave urgently. Another long day and overnight journey in the sampan brought them back to Macau. Wendy did not join them— she would not leave their grandmother, and would not come to America until after she died.

Having satisfied what she could of her promise to her father, Betty prepared to leave Hong Kong. But she suffered terribly, feeling she should have been able to arrange for Wendy's release from the mainland. Although a child herself, she felt she had somehow failed her father. And they had no word of her mother still imprisoned on the mainland.

Betty had help for her trip to San Francisco from the U.S. Embassy in Hong Kong. A social worker there arranged the rescheduled Pan Am flight. She dyed Betty's hair, which was growing out black against the white of malnutrition. She wanted to make sure that Betty was seen and cared for as a minor, and not mistaken for an elderly person. She gave Betty a twenty-dollar bill, a sack of rice, and a package of ramen. Betty also took with her the blanket that had been wrapped around her when she reached the shores of Hong Kong, and which she had placed on her father's body after his death.

Though gradually returning, her ability to speak was still limited. Her seatmate on the flight was a friendly American man in his fifties who was casually dressed and wore thong sandals on his feet. He helped Betty put her food into the overhead baggage bin. The simple kindness of this stranger impacted Betty deeply. As she traveled, she kept the blanket around her.

When she arrived at the San Francisco airport, Betty was met by her eldest sister, Faye. The music playing over the loudspeakers at the airport that day was unlike anything she had heard before, and the melody lodged within her; it was Simon and Garfunkel's "Bridge Over Troubled Water."

~

Faye was well established in San Francisco at that time. Faye's household included her husband, her own five children, and her mother-in-law. Betty stayed with this crowded family for a few weeks before traveling to Seattle, the home of her sister Pat and her American brother-in-law, Harold.

Betty slept in their laundry room for a time. Harold kindly provided a tiny TV that was propped on the washing machine. While her sister and brother-in-law were at work, Betty watched *Sesame Street* and *Mister Rogers' Neighborhood* and began to learn English. Months later, her brothers King and Michael, sufficiently recovered from TB to get clear health certificates, joined them. The boys both got jobs at a design firm, working hard and pooling their money until they could buy a small house two blocks from their sister's home. King, Michael, and Betty lived together there for a time.

Shortly after, Kathy and her husband joined them from Macau. They both worked two jobs, including washing dishes at a Chinese restaurant, and Betty babysat their sons. Kathy and her family lived with Pat and Harold for less than a year before saving enough money to buy their own two-bedroom house nearby.

Things settled into a new life for the four escaped Kwan siblings. They focused on gathering enough financial resources to buy and maintain property that would provide security and a home of their own. The terror of their recent experience became somewhat subsumed by the demands of improving their English, making their way in business, and becoming productive members of the growing Chinese American community in Seattle.

Having been so much younger than the other three escapees when their lives were shattered, Betty was in a difficult position. She had missed the training usually received in early school years. Now in her teens, she could not read either Cantonese characters (Hanzi) or the English alphabet, and could not easily be enrolled in a U.S. public school. With her siblings toiling for financial survival, there was neither time nor money to hire her a tutor. The family continued to speak Cantonese at home, but her inability to speak or read English hampered her integration into her new community. She felt like she was baggage, and that she belonged nowhere.

In addition, Betty suffered from an array of post-traumatic physical and emotional reactions. She had flashbacks, episodes of dissociation and amnesia, compulsions to run and hide, aversion to raw or uncooked foods and to wearing shoes, and pervasive distrust. At times, smells, noises, or even men's voices overwhelmed her. Smells of gasoline, barbecue, and human waste evoked strong visceral and emotional reactions. Her brain's internal danger signal was always on high alert. The idea that she was a Devil Child and therefore dangerous to anyone who might love her was deeply ingrained. Her whole being needed healing, but there were few resources to support the healing process.

The four children who escaped together shared a bond forged in anguish. They were part of a fellowship only they could understand. Even their eldest siblings knew little of the atrocities they had suffered. When Betty spoke of it to them, she was not sure if they believed her. She learned it was better to say nothing, a skill for which she had years of practice. Mostly, she wanted to forget, to move forward, and to build a new life far away from the dark memories.

Validation for the four escaped children came on the occasion of Alex's marriage in San Francisco. At the reception, the relative who had beaten Grandmother Kwan on the night of the raid was there and spoke with Betty's elder sister. The relative confessed to having engaged in the beating that night and said that they themselves would have been imprisoned if they had not joined in the denunciation of the family. This event opened an opportunity for the older and the younger children to speak together of things previously unsaid. Betty finally felt that there was some credibility given to her experience.[5]

But there were happier associations too. When Betty visited San Francisco's Chinatown, shop owners on Stockton and Powell Streets invited her to take whatever she wanted. "Your family was so good to my parents and my grandparents," they said. However, even these kindnesses underscored a continuing trouble. While these shopkeepers had successfully immigrated and were prospering, Betty's mother remained imprisoned on the Chinese mainland.

~

Long before the Cultural Revolution, Betty's mother treated a man dying of pneumonia. He had been traveling from another province with his young son when he became ill and found his way to her clinic. She was unable to save the traveler. His son, who was about four years old, had no other family. She took the boy in and raised him in the Kwan household, where he learned to speak Cantonese. When he was a teen, he disappeared without taking anything with him and without anyone knowing where he had gone. His disappearance was sad and unsettling to Betty's mother, who was fond of him.

Decades later, this man had become a powerful officer in the Chinese military, a four-star general, who reappeared suddenly in the family's life. After the end of the Cultural Revolution in 1976, he came to Kaiping looking for Tak-chui Kwan, and found that she had been imprisoned since 1967, when she had been given a twenty-five-year sentence. It is a part of the oral tradition of the family that he then went to visit her in prison and advocated for her release.

---

5 What happened was so unthinkable to those who had left before the Cultural Revolution that they could not comprehend it. Thousands who had escaped were profoundly frightened, traumatized, and ashamed. Many, including some of Betty's extended family, cannot or will not speak of their experiences to this day, and are reluctant for their children to know of it. Only recently have written accounts been published in the West, many detailing exactly the kinds of things Betty and her family suffered. These accounts are a sad but essential validation of the trauma those survivors endured. Some survivors continue to live in great fear of the Chinese government, anxious that its long reach could still harm them, even from such a distance.

The family also says that President Nixon specifically asked for Tak-chui Kwan's release, as an American citizen, in February 1976. Harold, Pat's husband, was an Arizona native who worked for Sen. Barry Goldwater for a time. It is said that he alerted Senator Goldwater to the dilemma of his wife's imprisoned mother, and that the senator made President Nixon aware of the situation. Reportedly, the Kwan family tragedy was on President Nixon's radar, and he made the request for her release during his second trip to China.

It is unknown whether this request was made and contributed to her being freed approximately a year later—or whether the influence of the four-star general on behalf of the woman who had sheltered him as a child had any effect. Perhaps it was the confluence of events that applied enough pressure to the Chinese government, newly reconfiguring itself as Mao grew ill and died, to create the conditions for her release.[6] If Tak-chui's former foster son had a hand in freeing her, Buddhists might say that this was karma, while Christians may see it as the principle of "you reap what you sow" at work.

Betty's mother was released to Hong Kong around 1978. She was escorted by guards across a bridge connecting the mainland with Hong Kong and through a gate that had apparently not been opened since the start of the Cultural Revolution. She was met on the other side by the wife of her nephew, who had been hidden in the family house of Sun Yat-sen in Macau throughout the Cultural Revolution.

Upon going to her Kowloon home, Tak-chui saw a large picture of her husband hanging in the living room and understood that he was dead. In Chinese culture, these large portraits are hung in memoriam. During her imprisonment, Betty's mother had never been told that her husband had died years before. When she saw the picture of Jack Kwan, she told her niece that she was glad he had died, because she would not have wanted him to know she had been raped, among other atrocities.

---

6 Mao died in September 1976, and Betty remembers it was some time after that her mother was released. The family history says she was imprisoned for more than ten years of her twenty-five-year sentence. This would have put her release date around 1977–78. It was not until 1979 that the U.S. recognized the People's Republic of China, rather than the Republic of China in Taiwan, as the legitimate seat of the Chinese government.

Betty's mother wanted to stay in Hong Kong and work on freeing her daughter Wendy and her mother-in-law, who were still living in Guangzhou. However, her husband's brother, George, was now the head of the family and wielded traditional family authority. He convinced her that the danger of trying to get Wendy and Grandmother Kwan out of the mainland was too great, and that her duty was now to her children in America. Because of her American citizenship, she was in a much better position to finalize the citizenship of her foreign-born children than their sister Faye was. A parent has a simpler and more straightforward application process on behalf of their children. George persuaded her that she must set her will to moving forward and helping them in America.

Tak-chui traveled to Faye's home in San Francisco where she helped finalize her children's citizenship applications and assisted with Faye's younger children. She did all that was required of her as matriarch, and participated in and was honored at family events, but she remained reserved and emotionally distant. Betty never heard her talk of anything that had happened to her during the Cultural Revolution. She told Betty how disturbed she was that she could not find tears to cry. Tak-chui's trauma seemed to have sealed off access to her own feelings. She did not talk about her ordeal, nor did she allow herself to reveal her emotions. Betty expressed great compassion and understanding for what her mother suffered and the desolate place to which that suffering brought her.

Even after more than ten years of imprisonment, Tak-chui's dissonance from traditional Chinese expectations was still remembered by the community. While in Faye's home in San Francisco, Tak-chui was criticized by the expatriate community for breaking traditions. Faye's home was a gathering place for Chinese Americans, and many remembered Dr. Kwan from Kaiping. They once told Faye of a scandal her mother had caused: a nanny and a male servant had a love affair, and Tak-chui allowed it. They should not have been allowed to be in the same room, let alone fall in love. The villagers had long memories for such scandals, but they also had long memories for the Kwan family's generosity and service. In San Francisco's Chinatown, few restaurant owners would let her family pay for a meal. They remembered the baskets of food in front of the Kwan house that had kept their parents and grandparents from starving.

Eventually, Faye needed less help with her children, and Tak-chui moved in with her other children in Seattle. Around 2005, while living in Seattle with her children, Tak-chui had severe gastrointestinal problems. Scans showed a mass, which the doctors thought might be colon cancer. Her longtime doctor refused to do surgery because she had scars all over her body and asked another doctor to do the operation. Surgery revealed that a mass of hair, sand, and rocks had grown into the muscle of her colon. These were the fossilized remains of what she had been forced to ingest in prison.[7]

Betty spent the night in the hospital with her mother as she recovered, and asked her about the torture she had suffered, hoping that her mother would open up a little. She also asked her to explain her label as a Devil Child. Betty wanted to understand, from the one person who knew the situation and outcome best, how and why she had come to carry this burden. But Betty's mother still refused to speak of what had happened to her or to Betty. All she would say was that she was sorry she had brought her ten children into the world only to suffer. Her mother's face was creased with guilt and grief, to which she would not or could not put further words.

After Dr. Kwan's resettlement in Seattle, a Chinese man who had emigrated while she was in prison came to see her. He had learned that the Kwan children had arranged to have Jack Kwan's interred bones moved from Hong Kong to a cemetery in Seattle, where he went first to pay his respects before going to speak with Tak-chui. He also admitted to having been one of the executioners of her son and daughter-in-law. He asked for her forgiveness. He was a member of the Red Guard and before the Cultural Revolution had been employed in one of Jack Kwan's restaurants.

Betty's mother forgave the man, telling him, "It is over. You were not under your own will, you were brainwashed." Even in her own desolation, she was able to extend grace to her former persecutor.

---

7 Medically, these masses of indigestible material are known as bezoars.

Chapter 10

A New Life

The Chinese expatriate community in Seattle was close and supportive of new arrivals, and it was natural that members of the community would begin thinking of matches between eligible singles. But for Betty, the thought of marriage was frightening as it meant exposing the scars, both physical and emotional, she had hidden for so long. She wanted to be like the blind girls in her Kaiping compound, most of whom were protected from the vulnerability of marriage.

But, inevitably, the Kwan family was introduced to the Chinn family,[1] who were by then well known in Seattle's Chinese American community. A good friend of Mrs. Chinn lived just a few blocks from Betty's sisters and brothers-in-law, and this woman became the link between the Kwans and the Chinns. Her son, Leung Chinn, was a likable, bookish man with a perceptive gaze and a kind, infectious smile. He had recently received his Ph.D. and begun work as a physics and mathematics professor at Humboldt State University in Northern California. And he was single.

The Kwan and Chinn families got to know each other, and from that friendship grew the idea that Betty and Leung might make a good team. In spite of Betty's reservations, she agreed to meet with him. It went well.

Leung's mother was always trying to set him up with her friends'

---

1   Leung Chinn's family history is described in more detail at the end of this book.

daughters, but he told her he didn't need her help. He had met "plenty of smart and good-looking girls," but no one that he felt was a match for him—until he met Betty. He said that in spite of differences in education, he felt they were compatible. It was not long before he became convinced that Betty was the one.

Leung said that while he was the one with the formal education, Betty had more education in Chinese culture, which was a plus. She would tell Leung "all the things you're supposed to do." He added with a hint of humor, "I didn't realize she was that stubborn." Leung concluded, "Betty had all the qualities I wanted in a wife. I was lucky; I made the right choice." And in Leung Chinn, Betty found a man with a dramatically different background with whom she nevertheless formed a complementary partnership and mutual respect.[2]

Leung and Betty met only five times in the year before their marriage. Their wedding was a large affair, given the Chinn family's prominence and the fact that Leung was the first in the Chinese American community in Seattle to receive a Ph.D. One of Betty's maternal aunts refused to attend the wedding, blaming her for the death of Grandmother Ng, the aunt's mother, because Betty had unwittingly led the Red Guard to the house where she was staying.

The newlyweds settled in Eureka, California, not far from Humboldt State University. In this marriage, a daughter of privilege who suffered enormous loss and was denied the opportunity for education came together with a son of poverty who gained education at the expense of much family sacrifice. At the wedding, one of Betty's brothers gave her four quarters. He told her to call him if she was ever in need, but there never was a need, for Leung and Betty created a good, new life together.

As Leung had been raised in Washington state since he was a small boy, he spoke little Chinese. Betty had been born and raised in China and spoke little English. They did not talk much in the first few years. By beginning married life without even a common language, Betty

---

2 The fact that Betty's siblings had been able to buy a home before her marriage was significant in that Betty would go into marriage from a home owned by the Kwan family. This was important to her brothers.

The wedding of Betty Kwan and Leung Chinn in Seattle, WA

and Leung had to learn great patience and persistence to become true partners.

After about a year of adjusting to life in Eureka as the wife of a professor, Betty became pregnant. She was still young, and although her English was improving, the language barrier remained an obstacle. There were few Chinese people in Humboldt, and having limited English, she could not yet readily develop relationships that went beyond pleasantries. Her elder sisters were far away. Leung, who carried a full teaching load, decided it might be best for Betty to have the company and support of her sisters as her pregnancy progressed, so they traveled to Seattle.

In spite of her family's best intentions, Betty felt shamed and unimportant in her return to Seattle. Sadly, she suffered a miscarriage with this child, a girl. Her brother-in-law took her to the hospital and picked her up, but during the sad event itself, she was alone. She could not communicate with the medical staff and she was frightened. She suffered medical complications after the miscarriage, so it was several weeks before she could return to Eureka, which she did by bus. Her first approach to motherhood ended in sorrow. She thought then that she was born alone and would die alone. The taint of the past seemed to be following her.

But she gathered herself. She invested herself in Humboldt County, and embarked with new energy upon the task of acculturation. Betty continued to watch *Sesame Street* to learn English. Her favorite character was Oscar the Grouch because he lived in a garbage can; she thought he could relate to her. She also continued to watch *Mister Rogers' Neighborhood*, and from him she not only learned more English but also how to tie her shoes. Once she learned to tie shoes, she began to want to wear something besides slip-ons.

~

Once Betty felt more at home in Eureka, she gravitated toward an art form that represented the secure part of her early life. She once again took up the Yue embroidery that her grandmother Kwan had painstakingly taught her so many years before. The art form was in her muscle memory and she began again easily. It was a way to reconnect with a beautiful part of her childhood, a time when she was allowed to run free with silk and thread.

Through embroidery, Betty could express enormous internal creativity and energy in form and color. Each piece was as clear and beautiful on the reverse side as on the front, with no visible knots of any kind. The pieces could be worn or displayed on either side, so perfect was the stitching. One piece alone boasted more than 120 different colors. Betty, as the artist, was free to choose the forms and colors, the attitude of the creatures portrayed, and their placement and interactions as an expression of her own imagination and feeling at the time of the artwork's creation. These works were therefore not only exquisitely beautiful but also emblematic; each piece was a historical representation of the artist's inner world at the time it was made. The pieces were unique.

One large piece, made soon after her marriage, shows a tree on

Yue embroidery, which Betty learned from her grandmother Kwan before age seven. Betty created this piece soon after her marriage. The peacock and peahen in the "tree of life" represent family. The rock in the water behind the birds on the bottom left depicts the rock to which she and her siblings clung when swimming Deep Bay.

the water's edge, with the sun rising behind it. In the scene, it is early morning and birds are flying over the water, walking on the ground, and roosting in a tree. The birds are in pairs, side by side but not "talking"— Betty herself was not yet talking much. A peacock and peahen form the central focus, representing marriage and roosting in the "family tree" in vivid color and detail. The birds on the ground seem to have a rather disjointed road on which to walk. Betty's own road was not perfectly clear at that time, but the colorful presentation symbolizes her lightening spirit and hope. In the water is a rock, like the rock to which she and her siblings clung when they were crossing Deep Bay.[3]

After the loss of her first pregnancy, Betty feared trying again. She eventually became pregnant a second time, and was constantly anxious about another miscarriage. However, all went well, and she gave birth to a healthy son. This was the most significant and hopeful occurrence of her life. Betty and Leung's first son, Lawrence, by his very presence, began to undo the Devil Child label that still tainted Betty's sense of self. Three years later, another healthy son, Stuart, was born. Becoming a mother was a fulfillment she had not dared

---

3 There are several other beautiful pieces, one of which is a large panel of bright pink silk on which Betty embroidered a dragon and phoenix, which are classic figures of Yue embroidery and important symbols in Chinese mythology. The phoenix is a feminine figure, and denotes that the article of embroidered clothing would be worn by a woman. The phoenix is said to symbolize virtue, duty, and resilience. The dragon was not fearsome but a positive figure in Chinese mythology, denoting protection, good fortune, wisdom, and nobility.

believe would ever come to her. It began to chip away at the sense of defectiveness and lack of worth she had internalized from her early suffering. Even though a part of her feared her childhood stigma might somehow contaminate them, her sons' obvious wholeness became a significant part of her healing.

By the time Stuart was born, Betty's mother had been in America for several years, and Betty invited her to Eureka for the birth. Tak-chui helped with the toddler Lawrence, and held and cared for the infant Stuart. Her mother was adept with the baby, which given her obstetrics experience was not a surprise. She showed Betty how to remove the drying umbilical cord, which Betty saved along with her son's lost baby teeth. Her mother's care was strong, efficient, disciplined, and reserved. Her presence was appreciated. However, while Betty had many warm memories of and feelings toward Papa, her relationship with her mother had always been more distant. Even then, that was no less true.

~

In her early years in Eureka, Betty began to explore the question of God. Who was God, and did an omnipotent God, or a good God, exist? What was God's nature? In spite of her mother's strong religious

Leung and Betty with baby Lawrence and both of Leung's brothers and their mother, at his mother's birthday celebration

convictions, Betty recalls hearing little about God before her family was shattered. She did not understand the taunts the Red Guard made both to her and her mother, asking why their God did not help them.

When her sons were small, she attended a class taught by the wife of a Lutheran minister, from whom she learned a great deal. She attended the Lutheran church for a few years before gravitating to the Catholic Church, where she found her spiritual home. She participated in the Rite of Christian Initiation of Adults (RCIA), a process preparing people to enter into first Eucharist and confirmation in the Catholic Church.[4]

A pivotal event in her spiritual life occurred when Ken and Linda Bareilles, who were members of Sacred Heart, a local Catholic church, invited Betty and her family to Thanksgiving dinner with them. From that simple act of hospitality, Betty was soon enfolded in that faith community. She attended the ecumenical Cursillo spiritual retreat, which further deepened her ties to her own local faith community. She became a beloved member of her parish and eventually of the diocese as well. A Cursillo retreat participant recalls that Betty had difficulty wearing the wooden name tag made for each person to hang around their necks. It recreated the feel of the wooden sign she wore for years as a child. The past was intruding on the present.

Once again Betty moved forward, focusing on the next thing required of her. She began to notice a thread running through her life, from her baptism by a Catholic priest, to the missionary sister cutting off her Devil Child sign, to the kindness of the nuns who comforted her as her father was dying in the hospital, and to the embrace of the Catholic community in Eureka.

The deep rhythms of faith became sustenance and strength for Betty.

---

4 The RCIA was facilitated by a person who remains a dear friend, Ann Lynch. Ann, who was a spiritual mentor for Betty, wrote of her, "Betty gives witness to all that is good in the human person. After living in the midst of such horrifying darkness and pain, she did not become infected by the evils she endured, but rather allowed herself, by the grace of God, to be transformed into an example of empathy, who provides light, healing, love and joy to those she meets." Another important spiritual adviser for Betty was Fr. Robert Benjamin, a priest who served a local parish. Betty long depended on his wisdom and kindness as an important friend and mentor.

Chapter 11

Betty Finds Her Calling

"The place God calls you to is the place where your deep gladness and the world's deep hunger meet."
– Frederick Buechner, *Wishful Thinking: A Seekers ABC*

"...that best portion of a good man's life, his little, nameless, unremembered acts of kindness and love."
– William Wordsworth, *Lyrical Ballads*

When Betty's sons began school, so, finally, did she. Lawrence entered kindergarten at Lafayette Elementary School, not too far from the Chinn house. Betty took Lawrence to school every day while Stuart came with her in his stroller. She began spending time at the school, keeping an eye on Lawrence. She was determined that her children would not endure any of the bullying she herself had experienced on the streets of Kaiping. Betty could often be seen walking around the school with her eyes cast down.[1] Her inward sense of shame and fear were still prominent but diminishing with the growth of her boys and the wholeness of their lives. At times, she still worried she might contaminate them with what she thought of as her Devil Child corruption. But her sons' undeniable health, intelligence, and vitality spoke against that.

---

1 From Lisa Bethune's unpublished interview notes with Betty in 2010.

She sometimes had episodes of overwhelming fear that would cause her extreme anxiety. She wanted to run and hide. Sometimes she did. She could not always pinpoint the trigger; it could be the smell of gasoline at a gas station, evoking the trauma of the immolated boy, or barbecue from a neighbor's grill, precipitating memories of her mother's branding, or the sight of raw food, repulsive to her after the diet of reptiles, leaves, and waste upon which she had survived. Sometimes the sounds of men's angry voices or seeing a police officer's weapon would provoke an episode of intense post-traumatic stress. These events were profoundly painful and disorienting for her. But increasingly her natural resilience and supportive community helped her through these emotions.

At Lafayette School, she deepened her relationships with children and staff; they created a healing environment. Students would run into her arms, warmed by her bright smile and kindness. Staff grew to respect her willingness to do whatever was needed, as well as her enthusiasm, perceptiveness, and reliability. Over time, friendships grew.

When Stuart began first grade, Betty was invited to volunteer in his classroom, her first regular experience of a structured learning environment. Betty was intimidated at first, but this exposure allowed her to improve her English and become familiar with the rhythms and tasks of American early education. Her dream of being able to attend school was finally being fulfilled through her children. With them, she honed her formerly rudimentary ability to read and write English. Betty began to devote more and more time to the school, eventually becoming a part-time aide and office worker. The loving acceptance that teachers and staff extended to Betty was a significant part of her feeling at home, both in the Eureka community and with herself.

As Betty grew more comfortable, she became known for her honesty and her ability to speak the truth in a kind way. Her dear friend described this trait in Betty, saying, "Betty had this amazing way of telling people the hard things that no one else felt comfortable saying, but that they needed to hear. And when Betty was done, those people would hug her and thank her for her honesty. Betty has this remarkable integrity that people pick up on right away. Betty always speaks her truth, but it comes from the heart in such a way that it is clear she is telling the truth."[2]

When Betty watched children throwing away untouched food, she would get a stomachache, an unconscious somatic reaction to waste by those who had never starved. One day, a boy threw away a wrapped, untouched burrito, and Betty went to catch it before it hit the bin. A cook later accused her of stealing the burrito. This accusation led to a traumatic flashback and Betty hid herself in the closet in the nurse's room, re-experiencing the feeling of the chain on her leg. The kind help provided to her at that time by the school counselor, Lynn Hartley, and the principal, Jim Sanders, led to lasting friendships. Kathy Honsal, later the principal at Lafayette, called Betty "the heart of the school."[3]

Betty's friend Lisa Bethune was a fourth grade teacher at Lafayette Elementary School during the 1990s. She found Betty's energy contagious, and felt that she had a gift for making everyone feel special. Even when Betty was a yard duty monitor, she would stay for eight hours a day, helping with PTA and track.[4]

Betty had numerous memories that would disturb her. Once, when she took her sons to a big tent circus in town, she heard the sound of the animal trainer's whip cracking at the animals, and she suddenly experienced a freezing sensation and could not move. "I felt like my spine was frozen," she later recalled. "I can see my tailbone to my neck, straight, like a stick, frozen like a bamboo stick with knots." Her body was reliving the night of the raid on her family home when the PLA whipped them mercilessly. Even now, the sound of a whip is intolerable to Betty.

In 2008, when Betty had been working at Lafayette Elementary for many years, a rock-climbing wall on the playground was dedicated to her. During the dedication ceremony, she was presented with a letter from Mr. McFeely, the postman from *Mister Rogers' Neighborhood*. Betty felt that Mr. Rogers taught her how to be a good mother because

2 A speech given by Lisa Bethune on May 15, 2015 at a fundraiser for the Day Center called "An Evening with Betty."
3 Thaddeus Greenson, "Betty Chinn," *Eureka Times-Standard*, October 18, 2008.
4 Mary Thibodeaux Lentz, "In Person: Second helping," *U.S. Catholic* 75, no. 6, June 2010: 35–36.

A letter from Mr. McFeely, the postman from Mister Rogers' Neighborhood, at Lafayette School

he was gentle, patient, and loving. When she watched the program, she felt he was talking just to her. She even used to hope that Mr. McFeely the mailman would bring her a letter someday. And he did.[5]

~

One day, during recess at Lafayette School, a small seven-year-old girl approached Betty on the playground. "Mrs. Chinn, I'm hungry," she said. Betty suggested she make sure she ate all her dinner.

The next day, the little girl told Betty there was no food at home, and in fact there was no home. The family of four lived in an old Chrysler Imperial station wagon. At night, they parked at the Montgomery Ward parking lot or under the Samoa Bridge.[6] Betty felt empathy and compassion in that moment. Her own wounds enabled her to perfectly understand the plight of this girl and her family.

Betty began to bring the student food from home. She encouraged the girl with her homework, giving her a quarter for each successfully completed assignment. The girl was bright and receptive; she earned a lot of quarters.

One Thanksgiving Day, Betty fulfilled the vow she had made to herself while living in the garbage dump: that she would serve the

---

5 *Eureka Reporter*, "Betty Chinn awarded log-awaited letter from Mr. McFeely of 'Mr. Roger's Neighborhood,'" September 20, 2008.
6 From a conversation with Lisa Bethune in 2016.

hungry on fine porcelain. On that day, no one in the girl's family went hungry. Betty served them on her Lenox wedding china under the Samoa Bridge. The father of the family was soon able to get a job at McDonald's. The family saved money and moved away. Decades later, Betty would meet this girl again under very different circumstances.

Betty's contact with this first family introduced her to a network of the unhoused who had been unknown to her until then. [7] She spent her small salary from the school to buy food for them. Her husband, Leung, contributed as well. She made sandwiches, usually peanut butter and jelly, or meat and cheese if she could afford it, and began to distribute them. She gave water, ponchos, and sleeping bags as she could. She did not talk about her work or ask anyone but Leung for help. She spent what she had. She felt compelled to give what she could because her own memories of deprivation, starvation, and hunger were ever-present. She also knew what it was like to be seen as inferior and unworthy. She had been treated like an animal for years while living in the garbage dump, and she knew what these unsheltered people felt when others looked at them with fear or scorn.

At first, when Betty's voice slowly returned during the months after her escape, she found she did not want to speak about her experiences at all. But later, she found it was important to describe what had happened to her. She learned, slowly, to give voice to it, and to see in another's eyes the sympathetic answer to her pain. In the recognition of others, she learned to see herself, and to understand the depth and form of what she had endured. It was a long process from confusion to clarity, and from resentment to forgiveness and a sense of self.

With every hungry person living in the sand dunes or ravines of Humboldt to whom she gave a sandwich, a bottle of water, and a hug, Betty felt herself healing. Every time she gave a coat, sleeping bag, or poncho to a person living under a group of trees, she felt her own

---

7 In this manuscript, unhoused was used to refer to those who are without stable housing. Betty herself uses the term "homeless," which was current when she began her work many decades ago. The now-preferred term "houseless" or "unhoused" acknowledges that those without housing can still create a sense of home, which is a broader term with emotional and relational nuances, not necessarily dependent upon physical space.

gaping wounds knit together a little more. She began to know that her suffering had not been wasted. Her pain had birthed her calling, had shaped a compassionate heart for the poor. She realized, after a near lifetime of feeling damaged and inadequate, that she had no need to be like anyone else. She had become at home in her own being. She said to herself, "I am Betty Chinn. That is my identity."

Betty had great trouble sleeping throughout her life, and used the wakeful hours to cook and sew for the needy. Sue Y. Lee Mossman, a friend and retired biology professor from Humboldt State University, remembers that when Betty first started work at Lafayette Elementary, she would retrieve the whole, uneaten oranges and apples that the students carelessly threw away and take them to the hungry. If the apples were soft and bruised, she made apple crisp or applesauce from them. If people donated clothes and socks that had holes in them, Betty would take them home and mend them before giving them to the people she served.[8]

~

The County of Humboldt to which Betty had moved with Leung as a young bride was quite different from anything she had known in China, or even Seattle. Eureka is 270 miles north of San Francisco, on the shore of Humboldt Bay, with twenty-five square miles of coastal estuary boasting a wide diversity of wildlife. The area is sparsely settled, dramatically beautiful, and foggy much of the time. It is on the major coastal highway from San Diego all the way to Oregon, so many people, both drifters and tourists, drive through. Some stay, many without any shelter, finding places in the thickly wooded ravines and sand dunes, where it is easy to remain hidden.

Like many rural communities once dependent primarily on natural resources, Humboldt County experienced a long, gradual economic shift. The two major industries in the area, logging and fishing, were both in decline when Betty began her charity. Logging of the vast

---

8   From an interview with Sue Y Lee Mossman on May 14, 2020.

tracts of redwoods had slowed for a number of reasons. People were becoming aware of the irreplaceable value of the redwoods that were thousands of years old.[9] The family-owned Pacific Lumber Company (PALCO) suffered a leveraged buyout in 1986 and eventually went into bankruptcy.[10] Many family-sustaining jobs were lost.

In the 1970s, over half of all fish consumed in California were caught in Humboldt Bay. But a decade later, a decline in salmon and ground fish stock led to increased regulations on both commercial and recreational fishermen.[11] In the face of this stringent management and regulation, many fishermen could no longer make a living. The global tension between economic prosperity and environmental sustainability was displayed in the microcosm of Humboldt. Some of the people Betty began to feed had been impacted by these shifts.

A third factor contributing to the unhoused population that Betty worked with was the ubiquity of marijuana farms. Humboldt and its neighboring counties made ideal places for the then-illicit farming because of the remoteness and sparsity of population. In the late summer and fall, young people would travel from all over the world to try their hand at lucrative "trimming" jobs harvesting marijuana plants into sellable product. This industry left some people without jobs or homes when the work was done for the season, and Betty helped many with bus and airline tickets home.

---

9 All but about 5 percent of the old growth had been cut down for timber by then, but protests successfully protected the last remnant.
10 PALCO managed its tracts of forest fairly conservatively, and while certainly a profit-driven business, PALCO cut selectively with an eye to the long picture. Then PALCO went public on the New York Stock Exchange, which made it fair game for being bought by majority stockholders. In 1986, the company was forced into a leveraged buy-out by Maxxam Corporation based in Texas. To service the debt on the highly leveraged buyout, logging was accelerated, and environmental protests ensued. In 2000, PALCO still employed 1,600 people. By 2008 when it was going into bankruptcy, it employed 350. The company went into Chapter 11 Bankruptcy, and was reorganized. The village of the company town of Scotia has since been sold house by house.
11 Caroline Pomeroy, Cynthia J. Thomson, and Melissa M. Stevens, *California's North Coast Fishing Communities Historical Perspective and Recent Trends: Eureka Fishing Community Profile*, UC San Diego: California Sea Grant College Program, November 2011.

Supplemental Information

Forgiveness

It would be untrue to say that forgiveness was a quick or easy process for Betty. As the deceased 1984 Nobel Peace Prize laureate and anti-apartheid activist Desmond Tutu said, "Forgiveness is not an effortless act for any of us and it does not serve anyone to minimize the complexity involved in the work of forgiving. ... Tell your story for as long as you need to. Name your hurts until they no longer pierce your heart. Grant forgiveness when you are ready to let go of a past that cannot be changed."[12]

What is evident in Betty is described well by author Parker J. Palmer. The true self is "the self with which we arrive on earth, the self that simply wants us to be who we are born to be--our mission is to live into the shape of true self, not the shape of someone else's life."[13]

There is an old Hasidic saying that describes this sense of being at home with oneself to which Betty had come: "Before his death, Rabbi Zusya said: 'In the world to come, they will not ask me, "Why were you not Moses?" They will ask me, "Why were you not Zusya?"[14]

---

12 Desmond Tutu, *The Book of Forgiving* (New York: HarperCollins, 2014), 38.
13 Parker J. Palmer, *On the Brink of Everything: Grace, Gravity, and Getting Old* (Oakland: Berrett-Koehler, 2018), 75.
14 Buber, Martin, *Tales of the Hasidim* (New York: Schocken Books, 1947).

Chapter 12

Two Steps Forward, One Step Back

"Great people come to serve, not to be served."
"How we do anything is how we do everything."
– Fr. Richard Rohr, *Falling Upward* and *The Universal Christ*

"I must be willing to give whatever it takes to do good to others. This
requires that I be willing to give until it hurts."
– Mother Teresa, *In the Heart of the World*

Some of the unsheltered people that Betty fed in the early years were just down on their luck in an economy with fewer jobs for skilled labor. Some were drifters wandering through on their way to somewhere else. Others were suffering from mental illness, alcoholism, or some other substance addiction. She began to go regularly, eventually daily, to bring food to small encampments throughout the county. She did not distinguish between those who were mentally ill or drug-addicted and those who had lost a job and could no longer pay rent. She simply knew they were hungry, and in doing for them what she had longed for and not received as a homeless child, she participated in her own healing.

An unhoused man named Andrew recounted, "Betty is so sweet and so honest. She didn't make me feel like I was being looked down on."

Betty said, "I just treat everyone the same. Like they are human beings; they are human. I don't judge them for being homeless or criminals, that's all they hear all their life. I don't tell them what to do, but if they want to change, I am there for them."[1]

Betty distinguished herself with the community she served by being utterly consistent. She did her work among the poor every day of the week, every week of the year. She treated each person with the same tenacity of love, honesty, and value.

The unhoused community began to trust her. She was unassuming and practical; she arrived with food but without an agenda; she did not want anything from them; and she gave whatever she had with a joyful simplicity. She was personable. She learned their names and then their stories. As she became more aware of their needs, she brought clothes, blankets, diapers, and other necessities. She gave out phone cards when someone needed to call home. She arranged medical care for the sick. She learned to serve without becoming embroiled in issues that she could not change.

When she observed children at the encampments who should have been in school, she began to pick them up in her van and take them to school in the morning. She arranged for them to shower first so they could be clean and attend school without embarrassment. She fed them breakfast. As the number of assisted children grew, she began to make multiple trips, starting very early in the morning. Betty gathered backpacks for those students at the beginning of the school year, making sure they were new and full of supplies. Many children whose education had been interrupted because their families had insecure access to transportation, adequate clothing, school supplies, or even hygiene were now able to get to school clean, fed, and prepared for class. Because Betty was denied an education, these children were especially close to her heart.

The unhoused people of Humboldt County became like another family to her. Because of her own experience, she did not feel superior to them, and as a result they did not feel inferior to her. And every day, she did what she could to meet the needs that constantly confronted her. She began by feeding a family of four and was eventually feeding

---

1   Gerdemann, Jon (Director). *Joy Makers*, Threesixzero Productions Pte Ltd., China, 2019.

Betty in her backyard surveying filled backpacks to give schoolchildren

hundreds a day. Because her work was motivated by empathy and compassion born of her own early deprivation, the people she served knew that for her it was not just a "job." It was clearly her calling.

~

As she expanded her ministry after both her sons left for college, the authorities took notice and informed Betty that she was not legally allowed to feed the hungry with food that was not prepared in a commercial kitchen. She could no longer bring food to the unhoused community that she had prepared in her own kitchen. This was a huge blow to Betty, whose passion and heart were totally given to cooking for and feeding these people. She felt desperately afraid that her feeding ministry would be shut down. Searching for answers, she approached local Presbyterian minister Rev. Dan Price, whom she called Pastor Dan. She asked if she could use the church's commercial kitchen. Pastor Dan was supportive, the council of the church was supportive, and Betty began to cook out of the kitchen of the First Presbyterian Church of Eureka. She was also offered the use of several other churches and nonprofit facilities at different times.

Pastor Dan had become familiar with Betty when she received a local award. He was a member of the Eureka Interfaith Fellowship, a group of ministers in Eureka from a variety of faiths and denominations. Every other year, this group awarded a Peacemaker Prize to a community member whose actions contributed to the well-being, justice, and reconciliation of the community. In 2002, Betty co-won this prize, having been nominated by members of her Catholic church community who knew of her work.

As she began to cook in the commercial kitchen setting, members from her own Catholic church and the host church helped her. The work of helping Betty by providing food, making sandwiches, and distributing them became a community-wide project as many other faith groups, service organizations, high schools, and scouting troops started to join in. Some people were able to help for a day, some for years. Some could give either money or food. The local St. Vincent de Paul Society was helpful and supportive and allowed Betty to use their parking lot as a central spot to distribute food. Every day, Betty could be seen in the large church kitchen with many loaves of bread fanned out on the stainless-steel counters, while cheese and meat, or more often peanut butter and jelly, were being spread by a group of volunteers. Betty would be chatting and laughing and encouraging the group. She quickly learned the names and stories of every volunteer, and she did not forget them. The people who volunteered regularly became a team and enjoyed being a part of Betty's circle of goodness and influence. Her light, joy, and generosity were infectious.

Leung began picking up donated food from restaurants every night so Betty could distribute it in the mornings. He often packed and unpacked the heavy catering dishes from her vehicle. This was especially important after Betty suffered a serious back injury. Leung's quiet, unassuming kindness was a constant presence. After his retirement, he expanded his role in Betty's ministry, and when asked to return to teaching temporarily, told the university that he was too busy working with his wife.

Leung worked quietly behind the scenes, not drawing attention but making himself available to pick up and drop off donated food and supplies almost every day, year after year, with a self-effacing grace.

Stuart Chinn said of his father, "He has been very good with Mom's work, not looking for credit. He doesn't need the limelight, but he does a lot to help."

But Betty was not without detractors. She was accused of enabling people to be irresponsible. She was accused of attracting them to the area because her generosity had become known. She was blamed for unhoused people congregating in the Old Town business district, harming the retail businesses there. These concerns were held by some people trying to find a balance between the needs of the houseless and the needs of businesses to engage in commerce without customers being scared away by those who lived rough and were sometimes disruptive and frightening. The argument about "enabling" made both her and her work a focus of the authorities. She was fined by the police. For a time, she was forbidden to even go to the Old Town district. Business owners were told to call the police if they saw Betty's red Dodge Caravan, which was what she loaded with coffee and sandwiches in those days.

This experience of being ostracized and separated as "less than" was terrifically painful for Betty. It was reminiscent of the years she was relegated to the garbage dump as a tortured and hungry child. Those who actually worked with Betty knew better. They saw her skill at discerning those who truly needed help from those who did not. They saw her reprimand disrespectful behavior. They saw her confront even scary, big men as though they were her children. One friend said, "To those that say that Betty enables the homeless, all I can say is that you haven't seen Betty in action."[2] Betty developed a tough-love style that garnered respect from the unhoused people she worked with. They could sense her deep compassion underneath her high expectations and no-nonsense approach.[3] She had no patience for intentional disrespect but enormous patience for true pain. Her own experience continually informed her relationships with the unsheltered.

The theologian Roger Newell pictured Betty's journey as a resurrection motif. He wrote this reflection on the resilience of her

2 From a speech given by Lisa Bethune on May 15, 2015 at a fundraiser for the Day Center called "An Evening with Betty."
3 Lisa Bethune, unpublished communications, 2020.

spirit: "The truth of her belovedness remained a silent presence within her, accompanying her into the darkness. So, if it's true her persecutors somehow managed to kill this presence for a day or two days even, it may have been Good Friday and Holy Saturday. But it couldn't last beyond two days, as it were. Easter was coming. And even then, it came in fits and starts, but it came. She is Easter's child."[4]

The local police officers began to harass Betty. Seeing themselves as agents of public order, which included keeping the rough crowd away from the business districts, and seeing Betty as somehow complicit in their presence, they regularly made her life difficult. Because of Betty's trauma with the Red Guard and the PLA, she was terrified of the sidearms carried by the police officers. On several occasions, two officers, each in their own squad car, pinned Betty in her parked car. They crowded their patrol cars so closely to either end of her car that she could not leave. Horrifying flashbacks ensued, hearkening back to her torture at the hands of uniformed PLA. Those episodes shook her to her core.

One day, Betty was telling Pastor Dan about the repeated harassment. The pastor was in the same Rotary Club as the Eureka police chief, and he asked Betty to accompany him to the police station to speak with the chief. Agreeing to this proposal cost Betty a great deal; she would have to enter the dragon's lair of a uniformed man with a gun. But with characteristic courage, she went.

Betty and Pastor Dan sat down with the police chief, who was at first stiff and reserved. Pastor Dan asked Betty to tell the chief some of her story. As she talked of her experiences in China during the Cultural Revolution, of her hunger and homelessness and abuse by armed soldiers, and her passion to help the hungry, the police chief began to soften, leaning forward and listening intently. By the end of their conversation, he was visibly moved. He ended the meeting by saying, "My officers have better things to do; they will not bother you again." And they didn't. In fact, the police chief became one of Betty's supporters. Pastor Dan said of Betty, "She is the most courageous and remarkable person I have ever known."

---

4 From private communication with Dr. Roger Newell on June 30, 2020.

Step by step, Betty established a reputation, creating around her a group who admired her work and her person. This community slowly became her protection, a kind of holding environment that supported the work only she could do, with resources others had to offer. She was increasingly carving out a space within Eureka and Humboldt County.

By this time, Betty was transporting her food twice a day to about eleven different locations throughout Humboldt County, sometimes leaving her vehicle to walk a quarter of a mile across sand dunes and through the forest to reach encampments. This was particularly difficult because of her chronic back pain and limitations caused by two separate events. The first was residual injuries from when the dog attacked her while she and her siblings were making their escape. The second was a severe disc injury she received when she stepped into a hole in the schoolyard while working. Betty opted to avoid surgery, but she required extensive physical therapy. Her early years of deprivation taught her to ignore pain and discomfort, but as evidence of how terrible this pain was, even those adaptations did not keep her from limping.[5]

As Betty's feeding program became more extensive and visible, she had to learn to deal with the scrutiny of being in the public sphere. This was difficult because of her natural reticence, her continuing bouts of PTSD, and her fear of authorities. When individuals continued to publicly accuse her of exacerbating the houseless problem in Humboldt County, it was very painful. She learned to let the feelings wash over her, and to keep devoting herself to her task. Eventually the outcomes of her work began to win over the elected officials and county employees charged with care of the unhoused. Those who observed her saw that she reached some people others could not; she had creative ways to get people off the streets and into shelters or apartments.

5　The writer Henri Nouwen popularized the term "Wounded Healer" in his book of the same name. In it he wrote, "The great illusion of leadership is to think that [wo]man can be led out of the desert by someone who has never been there ... who can take away suffering without entering it?" Nouwen was speaking of people like Betty when he observed, "We heal from our own wounds." Betty's incredible ability to extend loving kindness to the houseless is not possible in spite of her wounds but because of them. She is an example of the archetype of a Wounded Healer. Her suffering has created inner depths of compassion and empathy that result in an attuned response to those who suffer.

As the tide of opinion began to change, Betty began to speak at community gatherings and organizations. Her confidence grew, and her passion encouraged people to volunteer with her. Those who came to help saw Betty treat each unhoused person with equal care. They saw that she was not a pushover. At times, her help was met with abusive acting out. She set firm boundaries, and usually those at fault responded with improved behavior.

Betty said, "I love them. I am honest with them. I tell them, 'How much longer am I going to live on this earth? You've got to learn how to take care of yourselves.'"[6] But she was fair. The people she served mostly regarded her with implicit respect and love. She felt safe even out late at night, watched over by the community of the disenfranchised. When asked why she worked so wholeheartedly to pour out her life for the poor, Betty said, "They are my friends. They are my family."

When asked whether she was frightened that she might die on one of her daily trips out to the tough outdoor communities, Betty replied, "I've lived a full life. If I die when I'm doing my stuff for the people, that's fine."[7] She also said, "If it is my time to go, it is my time to go."[8]

On countless cold winter nights, she got into her car and went to the encampments to invite the coldest and weakest into her warm car, heaters blasting. She lay down in the bushes with dying people so they would not leave this world alone. On rainy nights, she went out with extra rain ponchos and blankets, worried about those she knew by name who were wet and cold. Some mentally ill individuals were so impaired that they would lie exposed in thin clothing on wickedly cold and wet nights, unable to help themselves. She would find those people and bring them into her car, warm them, give them a hot drink, and get them into dry clothes.

Betty was a teacher. When she saw the unhoused people whom she fed throwing their garbage in dumpsters belonging to local businesses, she reprimanded them, rented her own dumpster, and made sure the people she served used it. She provided brooms and trash cans and

6   Mike McPhate, "California Today: A One-Woman Lifeline for Eureka's Homeless," *The New York Times*, October 25, 2016.
7   Gerdemann, *Joy Makers,* 2019.
8   Lisa Bethune, unpublished communications, 2020.

Delivering food from the Blue Angel truck (Photo by Gary Todoroff)

trained the people she fed to clean around the feeding areas both before and after a meal. Betty made a weekly trip in her own vehicle to collect garbage bags from encampments and brought them to her dumpster. Her experience of life in a garbage dump made her acutely aware of cleanliness and order. She tried to teach this value to the people she served. And Betty taught a whole community how to care for their unhoused neighbors.

Eventually, Betty's need for more mobility in food delivery became obvious. The health department had made it clear that for her to continue to transport food over a distance, she needed a food-safe catering vehicle. In a community-wide effort in 2006, funds were raised to buy and equip a catering truck for Betty.[9] "Betty's Blue Angel," the shiny, dark blue truck with its large logo that said "Love, Hope, Faith, Charity," became a familiar sight all over Humboldt County. Individuals from across the community, civic organizations, and faith congregations had participated in the campaign and they all felt a stake in this wheeled mercy. They had a sense of pride seeing it drive by.

---

9 This effort was led by Sue Lee Mossman, in concert with the Eureka Interfaith Fellowship (EIF). Sue was instrumental in the campaigns to raise community money by word of mouth for two of Betty's most significant steps: buying the food catering truck and later establishing showers for the unhoused.

Supplemental Information

Death and Resurrection

In the spiritual literature of many faiths and traditions—particularly Christianity, with its central themes of death and resurrection— there are repeated mentions of humiliation and return, dying to live transformed, giving to receive, allowing one's scars to provide another's hope, and healing others from the depths of one's own wounds.

In 1567 in Toledo, Spain, a young Carmelite monk named Juan de la Cruz was working with Teresa of Ávila to reform their order and was imprisoned by his own seminary professors and brother monks. He was a threat to their institution because he sought to return the order to voluntary simplicity, service, charity, and poverty. He was placed in a wooden cell that had been a latrine. The space was so tiny that he could not lie down. He was removed from his cell twice a day, but only long enough to be flogged. He was kept there for nine months before a sympathetic guard aided his escape.[10]

St. John of the Cross, as he came to be known, experienced imprisonment and a sensory ordeal similar to that of the children in the garbage dump. Dr. James Finley says of the confinement of John of the Cross, "... in prison he found something within himself that can never be imprisoned."[11] The darkness led him into a deeper, subtler light. St. John went on to complete the reforms and, out of the darkness of prison, create some of the most sublime and authentic spiritual poetry and literature ever written.

---

10 Richard Rohr, "Prayer in Captivity," *Daily Meditations*, Center for Action and Contemplation, April 22, 2020.
11 James Finley, "Dialogue 3: The Ascent of Mount Carmel," *Turning to the Mystics* [podcast], Center for Action and Contemplation, April 26, 2021.

"Mother"

Betty's friend Sue Lee Mossman said, "No wonder some of them call her 'mother.' She is so resourceful in figuring out ways to be a teacher, not only to the houseless, but also to city and county officials." She explained Betty's unique gift in working with those who are unhoused in this way: "I can't do what Betty does; she has a gift for seeing the potential in people, and recognizing what is the first thing a houseless person or family needs to have, or to do, so they can begin to experience some small successes. And then Betty knows how to keep encouraging and supporting them so they have the courage to take the next step for the next bigger success, and on and on it goes until the individual or family eventually achieves independence. It takes long-term, persistent, individual attention and mentoring and time, which Betty offers. She has the ability to gauge when they're ready to move on and take their next step."[12]

---

12 Unpublished communications after Sue Lee Mossman interviewed Betty on May 14, 2020.

Chapter 13

The Art of Forgiveness

"Forgive and you will be forgiven."
– Jesus, Luke 6:37

"Forgiveness is not an occasional act; it is a permanent attitude."
– Martin Luther King, Jr. from his acceptance speech for the Nobel Peace
Prize, 1964

As Betty's work expanded in the community, she continued to live with the effects of her early torture and trauma. She remained perplexed and hurt by the lack of help she had received from extended family during her years of destitution in the garbage dump. She harbored feelings that she could not release.

Betty attended a family funeral, and at the reception she saw the relative who had "struggled against" Betty's grandmother and thrown Betty away from the door of their house when she came knocking with her dead little sister in her arms. In an act of grace, Betty greeted this person, and they talked of their present lives. Betty spoke of her career helping the houseless. As they talked, Betty felt her negative feelings subside, and the present came into clearer focus.

She told the relative that she now helped the poor because she knew what hunger was, and that her pain had shaped her calling. In saying this, Betty fully realized the truth of it. Without her suffering she could not have done what she was doing. When the relative told of their own family and children, Betty felt only happiness.

The relative told Betty, "I just want you to know that what I did was a matter of survival."

Betty said, "If you find peace with yourself that is fine with me. I don't talk about anybody but myself. I have no reason for revenge; what is done is done." In a demonstration of compassion, Betty ended by telling her relative, "It was not your fault."

Later, Betty and this relative had a long phone conversation. They expressed great concern for all that Betty had suffered. They talked about the number of people living on the streets, and of worry for Betty's safety in her work among the unhoused. Their conversation was open, warm, and mutually caring. The bonds of the shared experience between the two, although they were on different sides of the conflict, had, over the decades, come to unite rather than separate them. Betty no longer felt resentment or anger toward this person. She and her relative were both victims of a shadow bigger than either of them.

Betty found ways to deal with the ghosts of trauma as they emerged. One day while walking down a Eureka street, Betty saw a pair of shoes in a shop window that, but for the color, looked exactly like the ones her Grandmother Ng had been wearing when she hanged herself. Betty bought them and wears them as a way of claiming that memory and diffusing its painful power.

When she saw a bucket with seams that looked like the one in which she had been submerged in the well, she bought it and planted it with flowers, drawing out some pain from the memory. These symbolic gestures became acts of defiant courage.

~

When Betty's mother turned 100 years old in 2007, a large party was held in Seattle to celebrate. Her early career and longevity in the face of her suffering was recognized as remarkable. Many people traveled long distances to honor Tak-chui: a nephew traveled from Europe for the occasion and a Catholic priest traveled from England. He was the same priest who had come from Hong Kong to Kaiping to publicly baptize Betty as a one-month-old infant.

At that time, he had been young and newly trained at the seminary in Hong Kong. He was a Cantonese-speaking Chinese man who had followed the history of the family over the years. He heard about Betty being labeled a Devil Child because of the baptism he had performed and learned much of what had happened to the Kwan family during the time of the Cultural Revolution, when escapees from the mainland were swimming to Hong Kong with their heartbreaking stories. The not elderly priest apparently felt his part in that event deeply enough to have traveled over the Atlantic Ocean to attend Tak-chui's party.

After the celebration, he flew to Eureka to meet with Betty personally. They met at the Red Lion Inn, where the priest was staying. During their conversation, he asked Betty if she was angry about her public baptism, and whether she felt that her mother had allowed her to be a "sacrificial lamb." Betty reflected on his question and realized that she was not actually angry any longer. She had been, but somehow the passing years and her work with the poor had settled her resentment into forgiveness.

Betty did not see her suffering as exceptional among those who lived through the Cultural Revolution. She had moved on with life and was grateful. The priest commented on her husband and sons, and opined that had she stayed in China she would not have been able to marry. Because she bore the stigma of a Devil Child, no family would have allowed their son to marry her. The life she had in America, with her loving husband and thriving children, allowed her to have a family lineage.

Over their school years, Betty remained a constant presence at her sons' schools, volunteering her support and time in many clubs and activities. Even after her sons graduated from Eureka High School, she remained involved. She established a Kaiping/Eureka exchange, which brought fourteen students from Kaiping to Eureka with their teachers and principal for two weeks, and then sent fourteen Eureka students and their chaperones to Kaiping for two weeks. Betty has always looked for ways to bring people together, and in this exchange she was uniting her two worlds for the enrichment of American and Chinese students alike.

When her eldest son married, further healing took place. The wedding of Lawrence and his fiancée Amy at Grace Cathedral in San Francisco was a solemn, moving ceremony. The reception that followed in San Francisco's Chinatown was an elaborate, joyful demonstration of Chinese culture at its most beautiful. Every detail of the multi-course, traditional meal was exquisitely prepared and served. The bride and groom, through multiple costume changes and rituals, honored their parents and their guests. For the guests, it was an unforgettable gift.

When Amy and Lawrence's son, Benjamin, was born several years later, there was an even greater shift toward wholeness within Betty. In Chinese culture, complete adult respect and status are only fully conferred when one becomes a grandparent. In a traditional culture imbued with sacrosanct respect for ancestors, to become a grandparent means one will be remembered by posterity. A new kind of confidence and joy radiated from Betty after Benjamin was born. He served as an undeniable, triumphant symbol of her survival, and of the truth of the hope imparted by the gray bird.

~

Betty holding grandson Benjamin. The grandmother has the privilege of naming a grandchild, and Betty chose to honor Fr. Bob Benjamin. See a picture of Fr. Benjamin in the photographs section.

As Betty's mother's life drew to an end, the doctor who had treated her for twenty-five years was at her bedside in a Seattle hospital.[1] Tak-chui was 104 years old. A priest came to the hospital to administer the sacrament of anointing of the sick, and as the doctor gently turned her mother onto her side, the priest saw the brand of the cross that had been burned into her back. The doctor later told Betty how significant that moment had been for him as he witnessed the priest's reaction.

Her mother was hospitalized several times before her final illness, and Betty tried again to speak with her about those incidents of agony that her children had witnessed, but her mother refused. She told Betty, "I took the brand by myself." In the midst of her extreme torment, she apparently felt abandoned by God. By the time she was finally released from prison in the late 1970s, her mother had rejected the church, and perhaps her faith, entirely. Betty never heard her speak of faith, and recalled that her mother refused to enter a church building, even for the occasion of a nephew's wedding. The only exception was for the memorial service of her daughter Wendy, held at Sacred Heart Church in Eureka, which her mother attended at Betty's insistence. Tak-chui Kwan had no tears for her own daughter.

The icy defenses that enabled her to survive imprisonment and torture seemed impervious. When Betty talked with her about what she had experienced, she would only say, "It was all my fault. I had so many children, and all my children have suffered."

After the death of her mother in 2011, Betty received many calls and emails. One call was from a man now living in Canada, who had been in the PLA. He admitted he had been one of Tak-chui Kwan's torturers. He told Betty that he had been brainwashed and was under orders. He was looking for absolution for behavior he now deeply regretted. This news of her death stirred his remorse into action and caused him to reach out to Betty, who by that time was well known because of the awards she had received.

Another call was from a man with Hansen's disease (leprosy), whom her mother had treated. He was coming to Tak-chui's funeral with his

---

1 Betty's mother passed away on February 20, 2011.

grandson to honor the curative care he had been given. He warned Betty that he had no fingers on one hand and that the other arm was amputated above the elbow. He was also missing the tip of his nose, all damage that occurred before Betty's mom could arrest the disease. He was preparing Betty so that she would not be frightened when she saw him at the funeral. He told Betty that her mother had saved his life; he wanted to honor her.

While Betty and her mother had completely divergent life paths, Betty's similarity in character and motivation to her mother became evident over time. Though in the past Betty saw an unbridgeable gap between the two of them because she had no formal education and her mother was a medical professional, the similarities became clear: two women passionately focused on caring for the poor, the ill, the needy, and those rejected by their society. Both equipped with enormous energy and persistence, they performed their works of charity in the face of criticism and disapproval. Both shared the quality of caring more for their mission than their own comfort or safety. Both personalities were stubborn, tenacious, and driven. Finally, they both possessed an inner mandate that drove them to serve the poor. Betty said, "I see my mother in myself. [I too am] a woman of power."

Chapter 14

Public Recognition Comes Unbidden

"Hope must be born over and over again, for where there is love, there is hope."
— Ilia Delio, *The Unbearable Wholeness of Being: God, Evolution and the Power of Love*

"Great souls resemble the elements in their immensity. They absorb everything—pain, injustice, insult, folly—and give back decency and kindness."
— Roger Cohen *New York Times*, "Two Deaths and My Life"

"...great love and great suffering... are the universal, always available paths of transformation because they are the only things strong enough to take away the ego's pretensions."
— Richard Rohr, *The Universal Christ*

In 2008, Betty's life changed. For over 20 years she had reached deep into her heart for the loving hope that kept her constantly working on behalf of the poor. Her persistent service and kindness had made her something of a celebrity in the small town of Eureka. Ken Christiansen, an elder at the First Presbyterian Church, had heard of the Minerva Award given out every year by Maria Shriver, then-First Lady of California, and suggested the church nominate Betty. Pat Person, another parishioner who volunteered with Betty, took on the task of writing the narrative and compiling the extensive application packet to be submitted. That year Betty became one of five recipients of the annual award. Oprah Winfrey, accompanied by Maria Shriver, announced the honorees on her program, and suddenly Betty Chinn's name was known around the nation. It was not something she sought or wanted, and in fact the publicity was painful for her; she was far more comfortable doing her work in privacy.

The award was presented to Betty during the annual Women's Conference, which took place for each of the seven years that Governor Arnold Schwarzenegger was in office. When Betty stood on stage, in a fifteen-year-old outfit she had bought from the sales table at a local department store for less than ten dollars, she said, "I accept this award for the desperate people and the needy people. This is not about me. It's about them."

As she spoke, her face was infused with joy and also humility. While the other nominees, Billie Jean King, Louise Hay, Ivelise Markovits, and Gloria Steinem, were already rightfully renowned, Betty from Eureka, in her humble joy, moved the crowd to their feet in a standing ovation.

Maria Shriver later wrote, "Mother Theresa said, 'I'm a little pencil in the hand of a writing God, who is sending a love letter to the world.' That's how I see Betty Chinn. Her passionate work with the hungry and houseless in her community is a loving act with profound impact. We know that simple human kindness can indeed change lives because Betty Chinn shows us every day."

At the Minerva Awards, the famous Irish musician Bono presented and spoke of his charities fighting poverty and AIDS. Betty sat backstage with him for a time, not really knowing who he was or why he was famous. But she thought he was kind, and she noticed that he wore tinted glasses, so she asked him why. He told her he wore them because he was shy.[1]

Unbeknownst to Betty, a stylishly dressed and well-groomed woman in her forties had traveled to the amphitheater to watch her accept the award. Outwardly, this woman was an example of the American

---

1 In Bono's autobiography he describes a meeting between himself and the Pope, to whom Bono gave the tinted glasses which he was wearing. He explained that the glasses were necessitated by migraines which were later diagnosed as glaucoma. Bono, *Surrender, 40 Songs, One Story*, (New York: Alfred A. Knopf, 2022). 364.

Recipients of the Minerva Award posing with the musician Bono

dream: she had a successful professional career, owned a large, lovely home, and was happily married with children of her own. But as she sat watching Betty, she remembered herself as the seven-year-old houseless child who said, "Mrs. Chinn, I'm hungry." She recalled when Betty would bring sandwiches to her family while they lived in their Chrysler station wagon, sleeping in the Montgomery Ward parking lot or under the Samoa Bridge. She recalled that Betty had served them Thanksgiving dinner on fine china. Decades had passed since Betty's life work was launched by this hungry little girl's simple request on the Lafayette School playground.

That little girl had become a highly accomplished woman, but her own husband and children did not know of her previous experience with homelessness, and she feared they would find out. She carried a shame that Betty understood all too well. When insecurity, fear, and a sense of not belonging are implanted early in the developing psyche, it can take a lifetime to heal.

Over the course of several years, Betty and this woman began to speak. Eventually, she made a trip back to Eureka to meet with Betty and face the place where she had once been houseless. It was a trip motivated by both sadness and a need to put to rest the ghosts that still haunted her. She and Betty talked and cried together. Perhaps a door toward healing opened. From the window of her well-appointed hotel, she could see the bridge under which her family's car had once been parked.

~

After the celebration and finery of the Minerva Award, Betty went home to Eureka and prepared a prime rib dinner to share with the unhoused. She displayed her award and told them they shared it with her. As much as Betty appreciated the recognition and the extra support it would bring to her work, she felt it was a bit of an interruption to the important tasks that absorbed her.

With the Minerva Award came a grant of $25,000. Betty knew exactly what to do with it.

Not long before, when Betty was feeding the hungry from her truck, she had tried to give a hug to a gentleman in a wheelchair. He put up his hands and warned her away; he did not want her to touch him because he was afraid his smell would offend her. He told her that he had not been able to bathe, had soiled himself, and that she should not come close. He told her that he would arrange to bathe that night and would see her the next day.

The next day, Betty looked for him in her group of regulars but did not see him. Then she learned that the night before, he had gone to the bay to try to bathe himself, and he had drowned. From that moment, Betty was determined to provide a shower and laundry facility for those without houses; a place where they could shower and wash clothes in safety and privacy, and enjoy the basic human dignity of a clean body and clean clothes.

The Minerva Award provided the seed money for the shower facility that opened in April 2010. The Society of St. Vincent de Paul partnered with Betty at their building in downtown Eureka. Longtime board member and local educator Russ Shaddix helped bring about the partnership. To help Betty meet the $125,000 cost, more than 400 community members made donations. Local contractors, one of whom Betty fed for three years when he was on the streets and who was now employed, donated time and materials.[2] Local coffee company Jitter Bean named a roast "Betty's Blend" and gave the organization

---

2 Sue Lee Mossman fundraising letter for Betty's showers, 2009.

Ribbon cutting ceremony for the opening of the new shower facility with Maria Shriver at center (Photo by Gary Todoroff)

twenty-five percent of the proceeds. Scouting troops held bake sales. Faith communities and service organizations of all kinds made contributions. And Billie Jean King, a fellow 2008 honoree of the Minerva Awards, gave $5,000 to the effort.

Betty's slogan for the showers was, "Restoring dignity, one shower at a time."

One man interviewed just after showering at the facility said, "Clean clothes and a shower make you feel better about yourself; things don't feel so desperate."[3]

Initially, volunteers helped to staff it, cleaning after each use, handing out towels, washing clothes, and providing toiletries and clean underwear. Betty eventually employed the unhoused and recently housed to staff the showers. The facility had three stalls, one of which was wheelchair accessible. When the showers opened, Maria Shriver traveled to Eureka for the dedication and continued quietly to encourage Betty and her work.

The tide continued to turn among the business and community leaders in Eureka. Previously, every new step in her work had been met with some pushback and resistance by those who feared her attracting

---

3 Gerdemann, *Joy Makers,* 2019.

the unhoused to an already overrun county. But a pattern emerged: once business owners met and talked with Betty, their minds began to change. When they saw what actually happened around the sites she managed, former critics became supporters. Where once Betty's work was seen as a nuisance, now she was better understood and appreciated. The city manager, mayor, police chief, councilpersons, and business owners had all seen the effects of her perseverance and supported her.

As the showers opened, a once divided community came together around her work. The local hospital, Providence St. Joseph, began donating all of its extra cafeteria food to Betty's feeding program. In 2009, a hospital vice president said, "I look at Betty as the Sister Teresa of Humboldt County."[4]

Over the years, Betty and Leung acquired several rental properties. The rental income each month was given to her work with the poor, along with her monthly retirement checks. She has never received any salary for her work. One of Betty's sisters gave Betty a large gift in 2008, all of which went to her charity work (whose finances were then handled by the Humboldt Area Foundation). These are not things she talks about, but are important evidence of her dedication, and that of her husband, to her mission.

Once the shower facility opened, Betty quickly established a program for smooth usage and supervision. For those who needed showers, she no longer needed to arrange transportation to the homes of people she had previously helped. Now there was one central shower location, and many could find their way on their own.

Although the shower facility was finished, Betty was troubled by an insistent desire, which felt like a deep need, to have a wooden storage bench with a hinged lid to put outside the showers. She wanted the people who used the facility to have a place to sit and put on shoes and socks after bathing. A supporter purchased the bench, but the intensity of the desire puzzled her. Eventually, she realized that she wanted to recreate the kind of bench in which she had first been hidden by her

---

4 Thaddeus Greenson, "St. Joseph lends Betty Chinn a helping hand," *Eureka Times-Standard*, May 3, 2009.

father on the sampan on the Taijing River, the bench she was pulled out of to go back onto the dock and untie the boat. The bench she was looking at when the boat pulled away and she was abandoned to the terrors of the Cultural Revolution. Somehow, having such a bench at the showers was a way to bring that painful image full circle, and to make it a part of her healing.

It has been estimated that over four decades of Betty's feeding ministry she served four million meals.[5] For the first twenty years, she did it entirely on her own.

~

One of the first clients Betty served at the showers was a wheelchair-bound man in great distress. He could not move himself out of his wheelchair to use the toilet, let alone shower. Betty opened the showers especially for him, and she took the man into the handicapped stall. She showed him how to use the shower and believed from what he said that he could hold onto the handrail while showering. However, after some time passed and there was no sound of water running, Betty knocked on the door and asked what he needed. He admitted that he could not raise himself from his wheelchair. His pants were imprisoning him in a solid block of excrement. They were caked with months of waste and urine. He had tied off the ends of his pants to prevent the embarrassment of leakage.

Betty cut off his soiled clothing, threw away the clothes, and patiently cleaned his body of the putrefied, clinging waste, inch by inch. She scrubbed and soaped and rinsed him under the warm fresh water. She washed his long, salt-and-pepper hair and bearded face. She found that his legs were infested with maggots that had eaten into his

---

5 According to data kept by the volunteer coordinator, Lisa Bethune, in the year 2012 around twenty-one children were taken to school every day, thousands of showers provided to more than 500 people, several thousand bags of clothing sorted, 285 sleeping bags and 300 rain ponchos distributed, 246 bus tickets purchased, and 267 people assisted in returning home. Twenty-three individuals and thirty-one families were placed in permanent housing; and Betty spoke to seventy-two schools and community groups—all of this in addition to feeding hundreds of people twice a day. Numbers on total meals were provided by Betty Chinn on July 11, 2020, from Betty Kwan Chinn Foundation data.

flesh. As she cleaned them out, she was reminded of the time she was forced to sleep overnight in a coffin filled with maggots and would have given anything to be rid of her own foul clothes and able to clean her putrid body.

She sterilized his wheelchair. She toweled him dry and dressed him in clean, warm clothes. She gave him soft pajama bottoms so his raw wounds would be open to the air but not hurt by rough clothing. Then she put new tennis shoes on his feet. When he told her that he could not lean over to tie them, Betty got on her knees to tie them for him.

As she bent over his feet, she felt wet drops falling onto her head. The gentleman was crying; his tears were anointing her. When Betty looked into his face, she had a transformative moment: she saw the face of Jesus in the face of the houseless man. She felt this powerfully throughout her whole body, and in that moment, Betty experienced an inner consolation of courage. She was no longer afraid of anything. She knew that wherever she went, God was with her.

~

In 2009, CNN featured Betty in a holiday series called "Breakthrough Women." This series profiled women who had changed their communities by triumphing over hardship. Then–police chief Garr Nielsen was interviewed for the segment, his sincere praise a radical change from when Betty was harassed by local police.

Chief Nielsen said: "I believe that she is probably as perfect an example of altruism as you can find. I don't think she has any other agenda other than trying to help people out. For me, that is personally inspirational. This job that I have often makes us very cynical of people and their motives, and to be associated with someone like Betty, who is really doing remarkable good simply out of the goodness of her heart is, for me, refreshing. It kind of rekindles my faith in the goodness of people, and I'm proud to be associated with her."[6]

---

6 Thaddeus Greenson, "Holiday season special with Betty Chinn", *Eureka Times-Standard*, November 17, 2009.

Betty honored as the San Francisco Giant's representative at Major League Baseball's "All Stars Among Us" campaign

In the summer of 2010, Betty was voted the "Everyday Hero" for the San Francisco Giants. This award was part of the "All Stars Among Us" campaign sponsored by Major League Baseball and *People* magazine. Each of the thirty teams selected a "Hero," all of whom were present in Anaheim for the All-Star Game. In Betty's glee at that ball field experience, one could see child-like exuberance and delight that no trauma could extinguish.

In 2010, California Assemblymember Wesley Chesbro chose Betty as Woman of the Year for his district. With her typical reticence, she at

Betty receiving the California State Legislature's "Woman of the Year" award from California State Assemblyman Wes Chesbro

first refused, but was persuaded when Chesbro reminded her that she was a powerful example who could encourage others to do more.[7]

In 2013, a mainland Chinese news organization created a documentary about Betty. They talked to several formerly unhoused people who spoke of what Betty had done for them. One said simply that she had saved his life. Another, a recovering alcoholic who was now housed and employed, said, what changed it for him was realizing someone cared.

The documentary team followed her around Eureka for a day, and filmed her feeding the houseless with the help of County District Attorney Paul Gallegos and his family, interviewing several other unhoused people whose lives had been transformed. The interviewing team went with her into the bush encampments, even at nighttime when others seldom take the risk.[8]

~

Betty developed a network of formerly unhoused people whom she had helped and whom she could depend on when others were in need. The fall and winter of 2014 were especially brutal in Humboldt County, and on November 19, flooding was forecast; many encampments were in the tidal zone where waters could rise quickly and flood the tents. Betty set out to warn the unhoused community. She ended up moving approximately 100 people out of tents to higher ground. Then she set her network into motion. She called several people whom she had helped to get jobs and housing years before. They called others they knew who had once been unhoused and whose lives Betty had also touched. By mid-afternoon, fifty-one host families had opened their homes or garages, providing housing for all of the stranded people.

Betty checked in frequently with the hosts, providing them utility money and extra food, which fortuitously was available from a recent canned food drive. Betty let the hosts know that if their guests were disruptive, she would come get them. But an amazing thing happened:

---

7   Thaddeus Greenson, "Chesbro names Betty Chinn for annual Woman of the Year honor," *Eureka Times-Standard*, February 28, 2010.

8   Gerdemann, *Joy Makers,* 2019.

the hosts all knew what these refugees seeking shelter were feeling, and the storm refugees were mostly respectful of their new environment. They learned to help with chores, they cleaned up, and they made it work.

As Betty visited them, she was amazed at the change in appearance and presentation of the people who'd come out of the tidal zone that night. Although many lived with mental illness, they seemed more themselves somehow, and healthier. Removed from the harsh environment of their encampment, they were better able to access mental health services and more likely to take their medication. Betty expected the need for housing to last a week, but after a month, as storms continued, most of the unhoused were still being sheltered by others who had once been in their shoes. In the midst of a weather crisis, it became apparent that these storm refugees were being mentored. Some were even being taught how to manage whatever money they had so they did not have to return to their outdoor camps.

The hosts told Betty, "I've been in that place, and you pulled me out. Now it is our turn to pay it back."[9] By word of mouth, extra and shared rooms were found. By January, fifty-four of the original storm evacuees were in permanent housing. Betty had modeled her gift of compassion, and those who had been raised up by it were doing the same for others. Love multiplied.

Later that same winter, on a bitterly cold night, Betty was out in her van with the heater on high, inviting the unhoused in to warm up. She discovered a teenage girl huddled in the bushes. In the wet, frigid weather, the girl was wearing only sweatpants and a hoodie. She refused to come into the van, so Betty got out and heard her story. The girl was eleven weeks pregnant. When her mother found out she was pregnant, she told her she had to have an abortion or leave. When the girl refused an abortion, her mother put two outfits in a black plastic garbage bag, handed it to her daughter, and kicked her out.

The girl and her boyfriend had traveled a long way to Humboldt County, but he was not with her on this night. Betty asked for permission to call the girl's mother, and when she did, the mother said she did

---

9 Lisa Bethune documenting her conversation with Betty around the time of this event, unpublished communications, 2014.

not want to raise another child. She would not take her daughter back. So Betty tried the boyfriend's mother. After checking out Betty on the internet, this mother agreed to take the pregnant girl into her home with her son. Betty took the girl to the bus, still holding her plastic garbage bag. The bus driver would not let her on with the garbage bag, so Betty found a backpack in her car and gave it to the girl so she could carry her few clothes.[10] As with so many Betty helped, she never knew the end of this story. She only knew one pregnant girl was out of the cold and wet that night.

On March 11, 2011, a magnitude 9 earthquake and subsequent tsunami decimated northeastern Japan. The cataclysm sent a tsunami warning across the Pacific Ocean to the coast of Humboldt County. While most people scrambled to leave low-lying areas with their families and possessions, Betty thought of the unhoused living on the edges of the bay. She drove out to them, and gathered about seventy-five people in multiple trips in her van. She initially moved them to a warehouse and office facility located off of Highway 101. When a friend informed her that this building was also in the tsunami zone, Betty didn't know what to do. She checked her email and found that she had received a message from a couple who owned twenty acres of land in a higher area. They had heard of the urgent need and offered their property. The landowners also provided tents, sleeping bags, and a portable toilet for the refugees from the tsunami zone. For more than a month, this encampment became a small, safe community. The residents supervised themselves and each other, keeping things clean and orderly.

~

In 2015, police chief Andrew Mills, Betty's firm friend and supporter, let her know that the marsh area near the bay was soon going to be cleared out. This was an area where many unhoused people camped;[11] waste and trash were decimating the ecology of the marsh, and it was being reclaimed. A crisis resulted. Betty needed to move many people,

---

10 Lisa Bethune, unpublished communications, 2014.
11 Lisa Bethune, fundraiser speech at "An Evening with Betty", 2015.

starting with the families with children and then the single people. Betty and the police chief were concerned most urgently for the little ones. Chief Mills knew he needed Betty's help.

She began to count those families with children and to plan for their evacuation before police sweeps disrupted the tent community. This was one of the largest and most difficult projects Betty had undertaken because it involved twenty-seven families with children, all of whom were moved into housing within about one week. Tapping into her social capital, she called on friends to help with rent and landlords to rent to the houseless, some of whom had not been housed for a very long time. A number of churches provided funds that covered deposits and first month's rent. She had built up storage units full of donated furniture, kitchen goods, bedding, and supplies. Finding homes for each of the families, she and volunteers took family groups out of the marsh using college students' pickup trucks. As a way of encouraging the people to claim their new housing, she asked each family unit to pick the furniture they wanted. She did not want them to feel like guests in their home but to treat it as their own.

Early on, the struggle and agony of some of those families caused Betty to wonder if she was doing the right thing. To have moved so many families at one time into housing was an emotional and organizational task that stretched even Betty's prodigious energy. The skill set required to live in a home, to be subject to schedules and external expectations and job tasks, was entirely new for some and long unused for others. Many of them required immediate treatment for mental illness and addiction.

The first month was full of angst and uncertainty on the part of the newly housed. Some feared they weren't up to the task. Many lacked basic skills such as cooking, cleaning, and time and money management. Betty visited each family unit twice a week. She insisted that they eat a family meal together around the table. She taught some of them to cook, budget, and clean, and she encouraged them, assuring them she believed in them.

Humboldt County Behavioral Health and drug services partnered with Betty in the massive task. Gradually, most of the former marsh inhabitants became accustomed to living housed. Within four months,

Betty saw real change in their level of comfort and responsibility. Within a year, twenty-two of the families had at least one parent working full-time, and four others had part-time work.[12]

Because she already had a relationship with most of the families, they trusted her, and they slowly began to trust themselves. Many of the people whom Betty served were suffering from mental illness or substance abuse, and were unable to go to an established treatment site. Betty bridged that gap by going to the encampments where the unsheltered gathered and developing relationships with those whom others avoided. Building relationships was her secret weapon. It did not always result in success, but Betty offered them a chance.

For the single people whom Betty served, she turned to the same landowners who had offered their property four years before. She once again moved about 100 people to the inland hill property.[13] The catalyst was the ecological deterioration of the marsh, and also numerous reports of dangerous activities involving drugs, guns, and violence running rampant, necessitated a sweeping eviction by the police. Betty had housed families with children already, but many single men and women remained who were afraid for their safety. They wanted to leave, but had nowhere to go.

Betty engaged in a grand experiment in community-building. She asked each of the people who expressed interest in resettling three questions: Do you want to move? If you want to move with me, will you follow the rules I set? And, because sitting around would not be acceptable, what will you contribute each day? Betty was adamant that those who came would be willing to contribute work to the community and respect the property. She did not want them to think they would be given this for free; she wanted them to have a stake in what evolved.

Betty chose twenty people whom she knew well and issued them a challenge: they would commit themselves to leadership at the new encampment and serve as Betty's eyes and ears, since they would be living at a distance from town. She asked this core group to move into

---

12 Lisa Bethune, fundraiser speech at "An Evening with Betty", 2015.
13 This account, like others, was documented by Lisa Bethune (Bethune, unpublished communications, 2016).

homes offered up by formerly unhoused community members first. During this transition period of a few weeks to a month, they would contribute to the host household and begin to strengthen a sense of self that would enable them to serve others. Eighteen of the twenty accepted the challenge. Betty applauded the two who were honest enough to realize their own limits and decline, inviting them to join the larger group later and help as they could.

Eighteen leaders in training moved into host housing. In two weeks, sixteen were still there and demonstrated more self-esteem, confidence, and independence. After several more weeks, the core group went to the property, met with the landowners, and set up camp. Betty met with the neighbors to apprise them of what was happening. Then she brought the first group of forty-five people to the property. She offered tents and sleeping bags while the landowners provided portable toilets. Betty brought food regularly.

On the first day the larger group was gathered, Betty asked each person a set of questions while an assistant recorded their answers: How long have you been in Humboldt County? Why are you here? What is your plan? Where did you come from? Do you want to go home? For those who wanted to go home, Betty made phone calls to social services and nonprofits in their hometowns. She provided bus tickets home after organizations in their hometown agreed to house them. In the first six weeks, thirty-eight people went home. For months, Betty regularly called the people who had returned home to check on their progress.

When the weather became wet and cold in October, Betty moved another forty people to the inland hill property. The structure of leadership proved solid. Residents supported each other and abided by the rules. The camp was quiet, clean, peaceful, and safe. With Betty's encouragement and help, many of the hill residents were able to find jobs, and as they became employed, three or four at a time would agree to share rent and move into housing on their own. One man who was a native of Florida worked for four months to save enough for a ticket home. He told Betty that while he knew she would have provided him with a ticket, he wanted to do it himself. By May, Betty was able to close the camp, as people had moved home or found jobs and permanent housing. The experiment had succeeded beyond anyone's expectations.

Betty had a bold, some would say reckless, confidence in the people with whom she worked. In one case, she bought a Green Machine, a motorized lawn and garden maintenance tool, for a young man named Gary. She then found several friends to hire him for yard work. Gary found he liked the work and was good at it, and soon had many gardening jobs. He not only paid Betty back for the Green Machine but also bought a Green Machine for another unhoused man, and gave it to him so he "can also remember what it felt like to be a man and work." This process went on through ten Green Machines. Local pawn shops helped by selling the machines cheaply to "Betty's people." Gary moved to Oregon and started his own garden maintenance business, where he employed a number of people. He passed through Eureka a few years later, and sought Betty out to thank her for giving him a chance and her trust.[14]

Emergency situations often called Betty out of her brief bouts of sleep. These events became so common that she usually slept with her shoes on. One night in April 2020, when the COVID-19 pandemic was forcing her to refrain from hugging or standing near her unhoused friends, she received a call at midnight. A man with whom she had worked was calling her to say "thank you" and "goodbye." He was lying with his body half submerged in the cold ocean water at the jetty. He just wanted to tell Betty that her care had meant a lot to him before drowning himself.

Betty told him to do nothing until she got there. She drove out to the jetty. Finding him lying almost submerged, she slowly coaxed him out of the cold water, foot by foot. She talked to him, and told him she was listening to him, but could not hear him well. Betty asked him to move closer to her so that she could hear him better. As she slowly backed up, continuing to talk to him, he began to crawl out of the water toward her. When she felt that he was safely out of danger, she called 911, and an ambulance came for him. Over the decades of Betty's solidarity with the poor, she had honed a wisdom that told her when to reach out and when to back off.

---

14 Lisa Bethune, unpublished communications, 2014.

Chapter 15

International
Recognition

"All who exalt themselves will be humbled, and all who humble themselves
will be exalted."
– Matthew 23:12

"...And the end of all our exploring
Will be to arrive where we started
And know the place for the first time."
– T.S. Eliot[1], Little Gidding, *Four Quartets*

By 2010, Betty's name and work had spread well beyond Eureka,
all the way to Washington, D.C. She had little time for extraneous
conversations, hyper-focused as she was on the tasks that mattered to
her: feeding, arranging for care, and solving problems for those she
served.

On this particular day, she was absorbed in just such issues, feeding
people at a local motel that served the unhoused. Her phone rang,
and the caller said it was President Obama on the line. Betty, being
nobody's fool, said, "I am very busy; I am feeding people right now,"
and hung up. She had no time for pranksters. She thought perhaps it
was one of her sons.

President Obama then called Leung, and having convinced him
that it was actually the White House, Leung excitedly called Betty. "It
really is the President. You need to take this call."

---

1 T.S. Eliot, "Little Gidding," *Four Quartets*, 1943.

When they finally talked, President Obama told Betty that he was awarding her the Presidential Citizens Medal, the second-highest civilian award bestowed in the United States. It is conferred by the President "to an individual who has performed exemplary deeds or services for his or her country or fellow citizens." Surprised and a bit embarrassed, Betty asked the President why she should receive this award when "lots of people feed the poor." President Obama said he admired the way she had used her suffering for good. He also asked what her next goal was, and she told him that her dream was to build a center where people were not only fed but could have help to rise up, to return to society as functioning citizens.

Betty went to the nation's capital to receive the Presidential Citizens Medal. Leung and their sons, Lawrence and Stuart,[2] were there to hear President Obama say: "Betty Chinn found both her voice and her mission: aiding those without shelter on our own shores. Every day, starting before dawn, she loads up a truck and provides meals to the homeless as an expression of gratitude to the nation that welcomed her. The United States honors Betty Kwan Chinn for renewing America's promise by serving those in need."

Before the ceremony, Betty was given the privilege of a little time to walk alone with the president. He asked her what it was like, given her childhood experience of suffering and muteness, now to be walking and speaking with him. Betty respected President Obama and Michelle Obama as much as anyone she had ever known. It was therefore without any disrespect that she said, in her simple, straightforward manner, "It is no different than talking with my homeless people. It is all the same; we are all the same." Betty asked the president how he was doing, and he acknowledged that he had a difficult job.

Demonstrating his own virtue of humility, he invited her to pray for him, which she has done faithfully since their stroll together. She remained profoundly grateful for the honor given to her by President Obama. She said of him, "He is a very nice guy; I like him a lot."

After Betty received her medal, she spoke to a television interviewer

---

2 Refer to the appendices for Betty's sons' reactions to her work and her receiving the Presidential Citizens Medal.

August 4th, 2010, Betty receiving the Presidential Citizens Medal from President Barack Obama

from the opulence of the White House, face alight with joy and voice choked with tears:

"I am from Eureka, California. I am serving the homeless people in my community, who live in the bushes. I do this because I was homeless when I was a child, and nobody was there for me. But I am here for them. It's my way to thank my country for giving me my freedom. I do what I like to do; it is my passion. Today is really emotional for me, because when I was seven years old I carried a sign on my neck that said I was a child of the devil because of the Cultural Revolution. Now, today, I receive a medal from my president. That is really a miracle. I really appreciate America; I thank everybody who made it possible for me to be here. I would encourage anybody, no matter how big or how small, to use your gifts to benefit somebody less fortunate than you who needs your help and compassion. Get involved. Don't sit in the house and do nothing."[3]

One unexpected outcome of her award at the White House was the large number of Chinese media outlets that covered her, and the resultant Facebook and email messages she received from Chinese

3 From Betty's speech after the ceremony wherein she received the Presidential Citizens Medal from President Barack Obama on August 4, 2010.

people afterward, who expressed their pride and happiness in her accomplishments. Some told her that her work made them proud to be Chinese. Betty began to feel reconnected to her Chinese ethnicity and her past in a way that helped ease some of the pain her heart still carried. She wished she had retained more of her Cantonese language, so she could have spoken in more depth with some of them.

When Betty was asked to be featured in a chapter of the children's book *Girl Activist*, she asked why they were choosing her—there were "many people out there doing good things." But she recalled what President Obama told her when she received the Presidential Citizens Medal: "You have a voice. You have to speak up. This is not about Betty—Betty no longer belongs just to you."[4] She agreed to participate.

As soon as Betty returned from the White House, she again served a celebratory prime rib dinner for the unhoused and shared the award, passing it around for her unhoused "family" to see and hold. She told them that it was their award too. She moved from speaking with the president at the White House one day to cooking, feeding her community, and washing pots and pans until eleven o'clock in the evening the very next day. For her, it was a seamless transition.

~

In October of 2010, Betty accepted an invitation from P. J. Wong, the owner of Asia TV (ATV), to return to Hong Kong to receive the *Loving Hearts* award. This award was being given for the first time to ten people who bettered the world by their acts of compassion. The ceremony and awards were co-sponsored by the Hong Kong government and ATV. Because ATV media had covered Betty's receipt of the Presidential Citizens Medal, she had become widely known in Hong Kong and China. Betty and Leung traveled to Hong Kong together. It was her first trip back since she had immigrated to San Francisco as a partly mute, white-haired teen.

4 Thadeus Greenson, "Betty Chinn: Activist," *North Coast Journal*, August 29, 2019.

Betty Receiving the Loving Hearts award in Hong Kong

Hong Kong had changed over nearly five decades; it was larger, busier, and more modern. The channel over which she and her father took a ferry from Kowloon to Hong Kong Island for his treatments at St. Mary's Hospital was now mostly filled in and built over. On this trip, Betty could not visit the village where she and her siblings pulled themselves out of the water because it was now prohibited.[5]

Betty garnered a lot of attention on her visit to Hong Kong, thanks to her newfound fame and recognition. She met with the Governor of Hong Kong and spoke to four large groups of people, sharing her story and message of love. As always, in the midst of being feted and feasted, she found herself gravitating to the poor. She interacted with them, and in her typical warm way, she hugged one unhoused man. A photographer following her took a picture of this hug, which was on the front page of many Chinese mainland and Hong Kong newspapers the next day. Traditionally, Chinese people tend to be quite reserved with regard to physical touch, including hugs. In addition, they do not generally touch strangers, let alone the less fortunate, because of

---

5 Changes have occurred in the decades since Britain handed over rule of Hong Kong to China in 1997 and, more markedly, since the 2020 Hong Kong Security Law was enacted ("Hong Kong's New Security Law: Why it Scares People," BBC News, July 1, 2020). This law, according to Amnesty International, is so vague and broad that virtually anything could be deemed a threat to national security, leading to severe punishment ("Hong Kong: National security arrests over social media posts violate freedom of expression," Amnesty International, July 17, 2020).

While in Hong Kong, Betty sought out and fed the houseless. Her hugging of a houseless man was so shocking to local sensibilities, it ended up on the front page of Hong Kong papers.

fear that misfortune could be contagious. For Betty to hug a houseless stranger was seen as remarkable and newsworthy.

While in Hong Kong, Betty was also able to receive Communion from a Catholic priest at a local church. This held great meaning for her, believing as she does that her early survival, and life since, were part of divine grace. She was surprised that the churches there didn't seem to engage in much outreach to the poor. She remarked, "I don't read the Bible much, but I know it says to feed the poor and visit the sick. I'm not solving the problem; I'm there to show love and compassion."[6]

She also visited the hospital where her father received radiation and the St. Francis Hospital where he died. She thanked the staff for the help she and her father had received. She remembered her father's last days in that hospital; she was alone with him as he died but for the kindness of the nuns. She particularly remembered a nun from England who allowed her to lie on her father's chest as he was dying.

During this trip she was approached by a gentleman who had heard the story of her father carrying her as a baby in his arms as he led the procession at his own father's funeral in Kaiping. This action was so outlandish at that time that it was still recalled over five decades later.

Because her work with the poor was now so well known, a wealthy

---

6 From a conversation with Betty Chinn on October 24, 2010.

man offered to make a substantial donation. Betty thanked him but turned him down, saying, "You have your own poor in Hong Kong. Please use the money to take care of them."

For Betty, this return to Hong Kong was revelatory. She had thought of it as a place where she could never again belong. It was a place where her family legacy, their Kowloon home, and the promise of reunion with her father and the security that represented had all been ripped from her. But now, she realized that she had a place in her home culture and a voice with which to speak on behalf of the poor.

In fact, her journey into the depths of despair, and her solidarity with others in this position, has given her the freedom to be at home anywhere.

~

In 2011, Betty received an invitation that rivaled any of her other honors. She was invited to meet the Holy Father in Rome. Betty and Leung traveled to Jerusalem for ten days, and then to Rome to meet with Pope Benedict XVI. It was the highlight of her faith journey. She attended a large ceremony where she was invited on stage with her local pastor, Fr. Ismael Mora, who was representing the Diocese of Santa Rosa, California, along with many cardinals, bishops, and priests.

She also met with some of the sisters of St. Joseph of Orange, who established the local Eureka hospital in 1918 during the Spanish flu pandemic. She then traveled to Assisi, the birthplace of St. Francis (1182–1226), whose simple message of service to the poor had served as a model for her own work.

This interaction with the Roman home of Catholicism helped her understand her faith more deeply. She visited the Pope's summer home, with the flag flying to denote his being in residence, where she saw him walking around the local village in khakis and a polo shirt. Only the fact that he was followed by a guard gave away his identity, and as he chatted with villagers, he seemed to share a common humanity. This experience strengthened the thread of faith that has held her throughout her lifetime, from before she even knew how to name it.

In 2013, when Pope Benedict XVI retired, Jorge Mario Bergoglio became Pope Francis. In September 2015, Pope Francis made a trip to Washington, D.C., and Betty once again had the privilege of meeting a Pope. Betty's local bishop had arranged for her to represent the diocese, and so she took her seat with Catholic brothers and sisters from across the U.S. She had the opportunity to speak personally with the Pope, the Vicar of Christ. He took Betty's hands between his own, looked her in the eyes, and asked her how she would like him to pray for her. She asked, "Pray for the poor of my community, and for my board members."

Betty was in the presence of someone who claimed the name of, and carried the spirit of, St. Francis, her spiritual model. Betty said again, "How could this happen to me? How? Only God." While in Washington, D.C., Betty was also able to participate in a service at St. Francis Church, where she watched the Pope hold and pray for babies and speak with the poor. It touched her heart to see the simple authenticity of Pope Francis' love for the poor, and his focus on families.

~

In 1981, five years after Mao's death, the Chinese government publicly conceded that the Cultural Revolution was a catastrophe. The Chinese Communist Party (CCP) officially declared that the Cultural Revolution was "responsible for the most severe set-back and the heaviest losses suffered by the Party, the country, and the people since the founding of the People's Republic of China."[7] And in 1982, religious practice was legalized, though with strict limitations and control. Attempts were made to incorporate the numerous Chinese religious traditions and rituals into the official history, and to honor them as cultural treasures.

The CCP allowed little to be published about the Cultural Revolution, but the government made overtures to its expatriate community, some of whom had fled during that time. Betty's first return to mainland

---

7 "Resolution on Certain Questions in the History of Our Party since the Founding of the People's Republic of China," June 27, 1981, Wilson Center Digital Archive, Translation from *Beijing Review* 24, no. 27 (July 6, 1981): 10–39.

China since her departure as a child was in the context of one such official overture. The ceremony and award she received were part of the government's movement toward embracing the international community and especially the Chinese diaspora.

Since 2006, the You Bring Charm to the World Ceremony has annually honored Chinese expatriates making notable contributions in their fields. Betty was honored at the 2012–2013 ceremony, held on March 30, 2013, in the Anniversary Hall of Peking University in Beijing. A representative from UNICEF who had traveled from Paris presented Betty's award to her on stage. The little girl in the garbage dump could never have imagined herself at such a lavish event, wearing an elegant gown, standing on stage in a magnificent hall to be recognized by the international community and honored by her home country. Such an image would have been just a fantasy. And yet, there she was.

The protocol for the trip was complicated. Betty asked to bring a companion with her, and this request was essentially refused. She was told that her companion could fly to China with her, but then would have to spend the duration, five days, in their hotel room while Betty attended the ceremony and traveled to various sites around the Beijing area, accompanied by an official minder. So she traveled to China alone.

Betty receiving the "You Bring Charm to the World" award in Beijing, China

149

Betty brought a handful of rosaries with her. These were scrutinized at customs by suspicious agents charged with disallowing anything subversive. Betty showed them the "made in China" stamp on the back of each plastic rosary, and the agent let her keep them. She was later able to distribute them.

Upon arrival Betty was given 5,000 yuan, the equivalent of over $700, to have clothing made for her by the excellent local tailors or buy some of the beautiful artisan work on display in the shops. While this generosity would have delighted most people, Betty had other ideas about how to spend such a gift.

After the ceremony, Betty was given a car with a driver to take her to see the Great Wall of China. She brought her rosary with her, and while she walked on the wall she prayed. Betty also brought with her two important talismans emblematic of the way her life had changed since leaving China as a starving, tortured escapee: the Minerva Award trophy from California First Lady Maria Shriver and the Presidential Citizens Medal from President Barack Obama. Pictures taken by her driver of her on the Great Wall show a beaming Betty displaying both honors in an iconic Chinese setting. Betty brought these with her as a statement that her mistreatment as a child had not determined the course her life.

Later, Betty was able to find and meet with some of the poor, hidden out of sight though they were. Every community, and every country, has people living in poverty, but like many municipalities, the government made attempts to keep them away from the city center of Beijing, where travelers and tourists might see them. Yet it was common knowledge that, even in Beijing, many lived rough and could not afford housing, a condition not so different from the community Betty served at home.

It was cold and many people were without adequate blankets or food. She used the yuan the government had provided her to buy all the blankets and rice from a local shop and distribute them to the gathering group of cold and hungry people she met. When she had expended every last yuan and the shop had no more to sell, she got ready to leave. She saw a man without legs, a double amputee, pulling himself toward her. Because of his disability, he had not been able to get to her soon enough to obtain a blanket or rice. Before she left California, Leung had given her a twenty-dollar bill to buy food in airports on the long trip home. Betty gave it to the amputee.

Betty was given the opportunity to speak to a gathering of thousands of university students in Beijing. She told the students that each of them could learn to care for others, and that whatever else they accomplished, kindness and compassion should be an object of their striving. She told them her story and she talked about her life's work, which emerged from her suffering. In a culture where crying is seen as improper in public, many were in tears.

A young man wearing the uniform of the PLA stood to speak to her. That uniform represented the worst of Betty's terror; at their hands she had experienced brutal beatings, torture, and the loss of her home and family. Now someone in that same uniform stood before her and apologized, saying, "Madam Kwan, I am so sorry for what was done to you and to your family."

Betty had long ago forgiven her persecutors. She told this young man that he had no need to apologize, that everyone made mistakes, and that they must all go forward—as she had done. A picture taken at that event shows her standing with three uniformed PLA soldiers. In it, she is smiling. There is another picture of Betty taken at Tiananmen Square,

Betty visiting Tiananmen Square and the Great Wall, and posing with members of the People's Liberation Army at the awards event

the site where twelve million members of the Red Guard gathered at the start of the Cultural Revolution. In the photo, Betty stands undaunted, with a banner of Chairman Mao in the background.

~

During this trip, Betty visited another Chinese national treasure, the Forbidden City. From 1406 to 1912, it was the seat of the Imperial Government. More than one million pieces of artwork, as well as ancient documents and books, artifacts from imperial households, bronze, porcelain, ceramics, and jade have been housed there.[8] Some were removed by Chiang Kai-shek to Taiwan before the revolution that put Mao in power in 1949; some of those artifacts have since been returned. The Forbidden City suffered damage around 1949, but further loss was prevented during the Cultural Revolution because Premier Zhou Enlai, second in power to Chairman Mao, stationed an army battalion around the city. Through all the destruction of other priceless treasures, art, libraries, and documents during the Cultural Revolution, the Forbidden City was protected.

While there, Betty was ushered into a room that served as the workplace and home of a distinguished elder, who had lived there all his life except for the years of the Cultural Revolution. He was 94 years old at the time of her visit. He was one of only two surviving members of the last imperial line, the Qing Dynasty, which ruled in China until 1912. He too had been imprisoned and tortured during the Cultural Revolution. He and Betty shared with each other the scars on their ankles left by the chains that had bound them. Betty felt a deep resonance with this man, and was moved by his wise serenity and gentleness.

In his workshop were the tools of his calligraphy profession. Calligraphy is a distinctive art form, highly valued in China as a method of transmitting culture and values and also for its beauty and elegance. This elderly calligraphist worked on long sheets of precious rice paper

---

8 "Forbidden City," *Encyclopedia Britannica*, retrieved August 2, 2020.

bearing his personal watermark and official stamps reserved for his use alone. He wrote out two scrolls for Betty: one for her to keep and one for her to gift to another. On the scroll are four Chinese characters, written vertically. They read: **Blessing**, **Longevity**, **Good Health,** and **Peace**. Multiple smaller characters descending on the left side indicate the Chinese year, the writer's name, the location—Beijing, Forbidden City—and the writer's official stamp.

Supplemental Information

Spiritual Connection

Renowned China scholar and Pulitzer Prize winner Ian Johnson said in his book on the resurgence of religion in China: "...hundreds of millions of Chinese are consumed with doubt about their society and turning to religion and faith for answers that they do not find in the radically secular world constructed around them. They wonder what more there is to life than materialism and what makes a good life."[9] Johnson also said, "This longing for moral certitude is especially strong in China due to its history and tradition. For millennia, Chinese society was held together by the idea that laws alone cannot keep people together. Instead, philosophers like Confucius argued that society also needed shared values. Most Chinese still hold this view. For many, the answer is to engage in some form of spiritual practice: a religion, a way of life, a form of moral cultivation—things that will make their lives more meaningful and help change society."[10]

---

9 Johnson, *The Souls of China*, 16.
10 Ibid, 17.

Chapter 16

The Betty Kwan Chinn Homeless Foundation: The Day Center

"And I saw a river over which every soul must pass to reach the kingdom of heaven. And the name of that river was suffering. And I saw a boat which carries souls across the river, and the name of that boat was love."
– Attributed to St. John of the Cross

"You have not lived today until you have done something for someone who can never repay you."
– John Bunyan, *The Poetry of John Bunyan Vol. II*

After her return from China in 2013, Betty received an early morning call from the sheriff's department. A frightened Japanese woman in her late twenties had been found sleeping outside the courthouse. She did not speak fluent English, but Betty recognized her from the recent food distributions. Betty understood her enough to hear her say that she had been a victim of human trafficking. Betty asked for the woman's passport, copied it, and then contacted a Japanese agency in San Francisco. She was able to get this woman onto a bus to San Francisco that very morning. But when the agency interviewed the young woman later that day, they said she was not in fact a victim of human trafficking but was mentally ill, and that they could not help her. At Betty's request, rather than send her out to the streets, the agency put the woman on the next bus back to Eureka. The woman arrived at 10 o'clock at night, and Betty put her up in a motel.

Next, she got the woman's family contact information from the agency in San Francisco. She called her parents in Japan, and the woman's mother answered; she could not speak English, but she cried when she heard her daughter's name. Later, Betty was able to speak with the woman's father, who did speak English, and who explained that his daughter was healthy when she moved to California years before to attend Humboldt State University. He said his daughter had met and married a man who abused her; now, after many years, her mind seemed broken. He told Betty he wanted his daughter home.

Betty and Leung collected this woman from the motel at 3:30 a.m. to take her to the airport. Betty arranged the travel, with help from her nephew and friends in San Francisco, to make sure she boarded the correct flight and made it safely to her parents. Remaining in contact with the father, Betty learned that the ill woman was hospitalized for a long time. The father repaid the price of the plane ticket, and was grateful for the return of his daughter to her family and homeland.

It was out of hundreds of stories like hers that the Day Center was born.

The expansion of Betty's work was gradual and organic. As she steadily served her community over the years, more people took notice. Medical and dental professionals began volunteering their services. Community members bought bus tickets to reunite runaways with their families, or paid for hotel rooms for the very ill. Many gave her their used clothing, and began buying groceries to help with the meals which Betty, by then, provided twice a day to hundreds of people.

Over time, local landlords took notice and began allowing some tenants, vouched for by Betty, to rent apartments without the typical deposit of first and last month's rent. In 2011 alone, twenty-one families were housed through this arrangement. The following year, thirty families were moved off the streets and into housing. Furniture, kitchenware, bedding, and other supplies were provided by donations from local businesses, service and faith groups, and individuals. In 2012, ten pregnant girls were helped off the streets; three were able to reunite with their families and the other seven were housed when a donor paid several months of rent so they could be sheltered. Routinely, the community now came together to help Betty's work. But the need for a permanent Day Center, with multiple services under one roof, was growing increasingly obvious.

Betty's goal has always been "not a handout, but a hand up." In order to extend that hand, she needed one location coordinating many resources to help the unhoused reintegrate as productive members of society. Her vision for the center was a place that could be the hub of a network, where people could access social work services, medical and addiction services, job training, and placement resources. She also wanted a stable and secure setting where services to children could be offered. And, finally, she needed a commercial kitchen of her own from which to cook her twice-daily meals.

Because of the respect Betty had earned in the community, she quickly received the funds and support she needed to create such a place. Henry Trione, a donor who had once lived in Humboldt County and was involved with Catholic Charities in Santa Rosa, provided the money to buy the original center building in partnership with Catholic Charities. Prominent local contractors Kurt and Kim Kramer led the renovation. Many local businesses contributed building supplies, labor, fixtures, painting, a heating system, kitchen planning and building, and even a security system.[1] A group of young adults who had supported Betty since their teen years undertook the finishing and furnishing of the upstairs apartment.[2]

The Betty Kwan Chinn Center was dedicated on November 16, 2013. For the first several years, Catholic Charities helped with the programming until Betty took running the center more fully into her own hands.

This huge and comprehensive endeavor necessitated a nonprofit organization, including policies, procedures, management structures, and a board of directors. For someone who had worked virtually on her own for three decades, this was all new. Betty struggled in those uncharted waters while continuing to do her usual eighteen-hour days

---

1 Dean Langor and Design Air; Jack Rieke and Shafer's Ace Hardware; Duane Hagan and CDH painting; Elizabeth Adams and Andy Dicky; Chuck and Rick Petrusha and Advanced Security Systems; and many others.
2 Chase and Michelle Adams, Brandon and Janne Rasmussen, Greg and Lauren Vanderwall, and many other friends.

*The original board of the Betty Kwan Chinn Day Center
Top row L to R: Chuck Fernandez, Justin Zibel, Lisa Bethune, Kurt Kramer
Bottom row L to R: Dan Price, Betty Kwan Chinn, David Tyson
(Photo by Gary Todoroff)*

of work on behalf of the needy. However, Betty was able to enlist people skilled in the tasks that were not her strengths. Many who worked with Betty found her vision morally compelling and were happy to run the business aspects of her work so that she was free to continue her immediate and relational interventions, although now under the rubric of an organization.

When she opened the Day Center in 2013, she assembled a board of directors that included herself, long-term helper and volunteer coordinator Lisa Bethune, Pastor Dan, the City Manager, the District Attorney, and several prominent contractors. The board later grew to include the former president of Cal Poly Humboldt and the president of a local security company, as well as a former Day Center manager. No less important were the hundreds of community members who helped Betty in myriad ways. Several local politicians at the city and county level volunteered at the Betty Kwan Chinn Homeless Foundation. Rex Bohn, a county supervisor, served as an auctioneer for many charity auctions on behalf of the foundation.

~

The center's mission statement was simple: "To honor all humanity by providing direct responses to immediate needs and helping the homeless achieve the dignity needed to return to society as contributing

*Day Center opening
celebration (Photo by
Gary Todoroff)*

members." The Center's philosophy of care includes that "every person deserves the opportunity to change their life. Every person has a unique path. Every person should be treated with dignity, compassion, and respect."[3]

The staff at the Day Center now included a program manager, a case manager, a front desk attendant, and a kitchen assistant. In addition, two employees worked in the children's after-school program. Each enrollee at the Day Center was followed by a case manager who coordinated services to meet individual needs.

The Day Center offered a bank of ten computers; staff helped clients with accessing computers, writing résumés, and searching the web for opportunities. A constellation of paper stars filled the wall behind the computers, each one representing a client who had found a job, paid off fines, or obtained housing. The center provided phone and mail services. A GED Unit Recovery program worked with certified teachers to tutor clients toward obtaining their high school degree. They also helped clients obtain necessary lost identification papers such as social security cards and birth certificates. In every quarter, the Day Center registered about 100 new clients.

Every two months, the local judiciary convened a Homeless Court at the Day Center, which allowed fines to be converted into community

---

3 Betty Kwan Chinn Homeless Foundation website, https://www.bettychinn.org/, accessed January 2023.

The wall of stars above the computers at the Day Center. Each star represents a job found, housing secured or fines paid off.

service hours. Many new beginnings took root from this opportunity to clear minor legal infractions. A four-day class called Pathway to Payday provided interview skills, basic work habits, and hiring opportunities to graduates. The program brought in local employers to the Day Center to meet with formerly unhoused potential employees. A clothes closet offered clean attire for interviews and work.

There was a strong collaboration with Humboldt County services. A mobile medical team from the Open Door clinic came weekly. Humboldt County Behavioral Health provided ongoing, intensive services to many of Betty's clients. Public health nurses and social workers collaborated with Day Center case managers. Starting with just a few helpers without written procedures and policies, the program grew to twenty staff members in 2020, including case managers, grant writers, office managers, budget managers, and those who staffed the shelters and worked with the children.

Betty slept very little. She'd wake up well before dawn to make coffee and breakfast, load it on her truck, and head out to multiple stops. She then picked up students who didn't have access to a bus stop or otherwise might not make it to school. She provided a shower and breakfast if they needed it, and then dropped them off at their schools. By afternoon, in the midst of all the other work going on with the Betty Kwan Chinn Homeless Foundation, Betty cooked again, often with the help of a formerly unhoused client, packed the food, and hit the road to distribute. Local restaurants and caterers regularly contributed their extra food, which Betty quickly distributed.

In addition to the ongoing feeding program, over the five years from 2014 to 2019, the Day Center served a total of 3,387 clients.

~

On the premise that breaking the cycle of homelessness requires addressing the developmental needs of the very young, the center offered a broad array of children's services. The after-school program for kindergarten through fifth grade drew between fifteen and twenty children.[4] The focus was on making sure homework was understood and completed, but the program also included recreation, arts and crafts, singing, reading circles, computer skills, and social and hygiene skills. Volunteers helped paid staff with these endeavors and with field trips, which included activities such as ice skating and rock climbing.

The atmosphere in the children's area of the center was warm and bright. Children greeted each other as friends, with smiles and hugs, and staff and volunteers interacted with easy familiarity with the students. Small tables were circled by three or four children working with an adult on homework, usually math or reading. When the homework period ended, a volunteer would sometimes play guitar and sing songs with the kids. Many songs were soon memorized, and the singing was enthusiastic.

Kids took balls to the outdoor play yard for games of keep away and catch. Board games, art supplies, and supervised computer time were available once schoolwork was done. Shelves were lined with children's books, and some students gravitated to reading in their free time. Healthy snacks were available. Around five o'clock, the children who had not yet been picked up by parents gathered with staff around a long table for dinner, which was provided before the children went home to their apartments, motel rooms, or the family shelter. For many children, this felt like their extended family.

Betty provided a week-long summer camp activity for about twenty

---

4 At the time of writing in early 2022, the after-school children's program had been temporarily on hiatus due to the COVID-19 pandemic. It reopened in June 2022 as a summer day camp, and resumed full operation in Fall of 2022.

children. For some of these children, it was their first experience staying outdoors for fun. They experienced outdoor beauty, deep quiet, organized sports and games, singing, campfires, and storytelling. Some of the children spent the week camping on an organic farm where they picked the vegetables they ate for dinner and learned how to make herbal ointments out of the herb garden produce. Such camp experiences also served to bond the children in deeper friendship.

When school began in the fall, Betty provided more than 200 backpacks stuffed with supplies tailored to the age of each student. Numerous individuals, service clubs, and faith communities contributed. Because Betty knew most of the recipients personally, she often customized the supplies and even included extra clothing, tagging the backpack with the child's name. Betty said, "I know what kind of clothes they like and all that...I want them to feel like they have more than everyone else for a change."[5] Inside was a note reminding the child that they are loved. This enabled the children to begin school with confidence and dignity, unworried about having adequate clothes or supplies.

With the official children's services operating five days a week, there was more opportunity for mentoring. One family had their three school-aged children in the program almost since its beginning. They had first come to the program while living in a motel room. The mother struggled with substance abuse, and the children's fathers were not consistently involved. Their loving grandmother, who lived in the motel with them, worked full-time to support them. Betty helped them to find a house and stabilize their lives. In the process, the children discovered how smart they were, and that they could plan for a future that included independence, with vocations that mattered. The eldest girl decided to become a math teacher after she found out she was good at math during the after-school tutoring program. The eldest boy, realizing his own talent and potential, moved from behavioral disruption to calm and confident interactions. And the younger daughter became more confident as well.

---

5 Thadeus Greenson, "'You are loved': Betty Chinn and volunteers ensure first day of school is special for homeless youths," *Eureka Times-Standard*. August 21, 2009.

Betty's long-term commitment made a difference in this family. The children had a sense of "home," not only with their grandmother but also at the center, where Betty and the regular volunteers enfolded them in a warm emotional embrace. It was clear how much she loved them, and how much they loved her. They respected and trusted her, and she expected good behavior, completed homework, and good attitudes from them. Because they trusted her, they delivered on those expectations.

Christmas time was especially important to the children. Betty partnered with the local police department to pair a child and an officer for a morning together, where they ate breakfast and then went shopping for up to $100 at Target. The money for the gift cards was raised locally, and the children had the valuable experience of befriending a uniformed officer, and of actually being able to choose whatever they wanted to buy. Betty wanted the children to know they were special. And she wanted them to know they did not have to fear a uniformed officer the way she once did.

Betty also served annual Thanksgiving and Christmas dinners, which were attended by the center families and open to the community. At the Christmas party, Santa Claus showed up for hugs and pictures. There was music, knitted hats and scarves (locally made and donated) for everyone, and, of course, toys in abundance for the children. Piles of donated new socks, underwear, and mittens were also available for the taking. Betty had become a mother to both children and adults who came within her sphere of nurture.

Betty, denied an education herself, was not going to sit by and watch that happen for these children. Year after year, she got up early, rousted the children, took some for showers, fed them breakfast, and then dropped them off at their schools. The need for a Day Center grew partly from her frustration that some of these same children had no safe and secure place to go after school, where they could do their homework and eat healthy food.

Betty regularly took junior high and ninth grade children to the graduation ceremonies at the local community and state colleges to plant in them a vision for their own college education. One day, Betty received an invitation to the commencement ceremony of a Ph.D.

student from a University of California campus. The name on the invitation brought her mind back to a little boy she had helped when he was very young. He had great difficulty in school because his nose ran uncontrollably, and he sometimes soiled himself. Betty helped clean him up and comforted him, and while doing so she instilled a message of hope in him. He would tell her that he was lonely, and that "nobody liked him." Betty remembered when she, dirty and lonely herself, felt disliked and unworthy. She told the little boy over and over, "You will be somebody someday, you will have an identity; like I am Betty Chinn, you will have an identity too. You will BE somebody."

Betty lost touch with him when he moved after fourth grade. That little boy ended up in thirteen different foster homes. In the last home, he was finally diagnosed with a sinus condition that had caused his constant runny nose; it was surgically repaired.

After graduating high school, he went into the military. When he had served out his commitment, he used the G.I. Bill to go to college. He remembered Betty telling him that he would "be somebody," and her voice became his motivation. He knew that to fulfill her belief in him, he would have to become educated. After receiving his Ph.D., he went on to teach in the California State University system.

When Betty received a wedding invitation from him, she reminded him that he did not need to be obligated to her. She told him, "You have freed yourself. I am so happy for what has happened to you, and I will always welcome hearing from you, but I do not want to be baggage to you. You freed yourself."[6]

After the publicity of the Minerva Award, Betty was approached by anonymous donors who offered to fully cover college tuition for needy students; many have benefited from this generosity. Since these scholarships began, Betty has sent an average of twenty students per year to college. Betty chose these students carefully from among those who lived in tents, cars, or under bridges. Children and teens who expressed interest in college were told they must attend school faithfully, do their

---

6 From a conversation with Betty Chinn on May 24, 2020.

homework, and make good grades. By their junior year, it was clear who was on course; those students were ushered into college after high school graduation with four years of tuition fully paid. One student attended the University of California (UC) Berkeley, another went to UC Irvine, and several attended Ivy League universities.

When Betty took children to the airport for their flights to their universities, she always told them that they did not need to keep in contact, that they were free of any obligation. Some stayed in touch. Some did not. She held them all in her heart.

One such child whom Betty had transported to school from a marsh tent was accepted at an elite east coast university. In three years, this student had finished all college coursework, taken the MCAT, and applied to the Johns Hopkins University School of Medicine. While Betty had not heard from him for some time, she received a call from the admissions committee of the medical school as they were reviewing applications. He had mentioned Betty in his admissions essay. A member of the committee looked Betty up and reached out to learn more. That young doctor now practices as a physician on the East Coast.[7]

---

7 Ibid.

Chapter 17

The Vision Expands

"The purpose of life is not to be happy—but to matter, to be productive, to be useful, to have it make some difference that you lived at all."
– Leo Rosten, address at the National Book Awards in New York, 1962

"The understanding that neighbor includes the other, the outsider, the outcast, the last, the least, the lost, the disgraced, the dispossessed, and the enemy … to love neighbor as oneself leads to the realization that oneself and one's neighbor are actually distinct yet inseparable realities."
– Brian McLaren, Daily Meditations, January 3, 2022

A few years after the Betty Kwan Chinn Day Center opened, a two-story building next door became vacant. Funds were raised to buy it, and this became the Betty's House Family Shelter. Both the Family Shelter and Betty's Blue Angel Village, a transitional facility housing up to forty formerly unhoused people, opened their doors by late 2016. These were the next logical extensions of Betty's community experiment. When Betty officially opened the Family Shelter in January 2017, Maria Shriver said of her, "Betty is the architect in rebuilding the family."[1]

Each new facility was met with initial pushback by some neighbors and business owners, and then almost universal acceptance when they saw that the sites were orderly, clean, well run, and not encampments

---

1   From a conversation with Betty Chinn on May 24, 2020.

Betty's House Family Shelter

but rather transitional facilities. Many of the same local businesses and contractors once again generously provided supplies, workers, and furniture in what became known as Betty's House or the Family Shelter.

In partnership with St. Joseph Hospital, the lower floor of the Family Shelter was devoted to post-hospitalization care for up to ten patients who were discharged from inpatient hospitalization without housing. The need for such a respite had become startlingly clear to Betty during the many times she found ill and dying people in the bushes with nowhere to go. This respite allowed twenty-one days of post-hospitalization recovery, during which the St. Joseph Health Care Transitions Team provided medical care and case management. As of 2021, 160 patients had stayed for up to three weeks. Some patients on chemotherapy stayed longer. And for some patients, it served as a hospice.

The first patient Betty walked beside toward death at the respite shelter was a man of British origins, without family or funds. He had been living on the street when he was diagnosed with pancreatic cancer. When he came to Betty after treatment at St. Joseph Hospital, he was in the end stage of his disease. Betty watched him weaken, eat less and less, and have trouble moving from his bed. Betty herself served his personal needs, including hydration and food, because she did not believe it was fair to ask her staff to provide hospice care. A nurse came daily, but he needed help around the clock. Because the man had no money or family, and beds for the indigent were limited, he could not access local facilities.

Betty came to know this gentleman and was impressed by his lack of fear in the face of death. She saw that death could be beautiful. He was calm and always grateful. On his last day, he asked Betty to call an ambulance and told her he would not be coming back. He reached for her hand as they awaited the medics, and he recited the entirety of the Lord's Prayer. Even the firemen who originally helped him and the ambulance drivers who transported him to the hospital were affected by his dignity, grace, and lack of fear. Staff at the respite shelter were likewise touched when the dying man told them, "Don't feel bad for me. I am going to a better place."

He was taken to the hospital and a few hours later his doctor called Betty to tell her that he had died. This man taught Betty a lesson about dying with grace and dignity, and possessed such noble character that he lifted those helping him. But some continued to die cold and alone and untended in the bushes, where their bodies were later discovered. They deserved better.

The upstairs floor of the Family Shelter had thirty-two beds for up to fourteen families with children to live together. There were separate bedrooms and suites with a shared kitchen. The transitional facility was designed to give families and children a chance to stabilize and access medical and psychological help through social services. It was the only local facility that allowed both parents to live with their children, rather than separating the father from the mother and children.

The Family Shelter was designed for six-month stays. Adult residents had to be employed or actively seeking employment, and children had to be enrolled in and attending school. Residents were required to attend all case management meetings, meet their agreed-upon goals, and actively seek housing. Many people could not stay housed because they hadn't learned yet how to manage their finances; residents also had to attend a weekly "money meeting" where they learned how to manage money, budget, set savings goals, and plan ahead. Residents set weekly savings goals for which they were accountable within the group. This instruction and support provided residents a crucial tool for independent living.

Another long-term housing unit was available in the main Day Center building itself, on its second floor, which provided transitional housing for specially selected clients who could benefit from more intensive mentoring. Residents here were taught skills to enable a transition to employment and housing, including money management, education, health, and communication skills. From its opening until mid-2020, the Family Shelter served fifty-one families, each with a stay of about six months as they transitioned to employment and permanent housing.

One family housed at the Family Shelter had four children. When the parents came to Betty for help, they had only two of their children with them; the other two lived with a grandparent. Betty knew the damage caused by children being separated from their parents—she still carried the memory of being alone and bereft without her parents or siblings at the garbage dump. She insisted that the other children be brought to Eureka so the family of six could move into the shelter as a unit. Made whole and given resources to help them move toward independence, one could see hope and joy in their faces.[2] As of 2022, that family had been in their own housing for several years and both parents were employed. When Betty offered them the gift of a holiday ham, they declined, saying they were doing well and she should give it to someone in need.[3]

~

The idea for a transitional village also grew out of the police sweep of the local marsh in 2015. Many business owners and community members feared that the displaced campers would descend on the business districts, making an already difficult problem worse. In an

2 Gerdemann, *Joy Makers,* 2019.
3 As of May 2022, per a private conversation with Betty Chinn.

unlikely partnership, a group of local businesspeople approached Betty with an offer to buy and renovate shelters and help her find a location if she would manage the site. Betty readily agreed.

The City of Eureka eventually provided a space for the Betty's Blue Angel Village about a mile from the main Day Center, demonstrating a growing spirit of collaboration with Betty. The Village was surrounded by a tall gated fence, and only residents, professional helpers, and staff were allowed in. The grounds were immaculate. There were benches and numerous planter boxes filled with sunflowers, creeping roses, bright annuals, and vegetables in a riot of color and green. There were picnic tables in the sun and a glass-doored mini-library full of books and games. There was a feeling of quiet, order, and peace on the grounds.

Five Conex (Container Express) shipping containers were donated and renovated and served as housing for up to forty people. Several of the units were combined to provide housing for couples. The units were small, clean, and private. Betty said, "They are a training ground to help people to learn to live in a house." In its first three years, from 2016 to

The arrival of the shipping containers which would become Betty's Blue Angle Village

2019, the Village served 726 people.[4] People invited into this program could stay for up to ninety days, during which time they received intensive case management services with the goal of transitioning them to permanent housing.

The Village was staffed by a program manager and a case manager. In addition, two program support specialists were on campus overnight. It was available to the chronically unhoused, with a specific goal to transition those who have been without housing the longest into permanent shelter. Humboldt County Behavioral Health and local drug recovery services also worked with Village staff reciprocally and cooperatively to provide services and care to residents. The Open Door Clinic's mobile medical unit came weekly to attend to medical needs.

Andy Pham, the program manager at the Village for three years, said the hardest thing for him was closure. Staff often did not know the end of their clients' stories because the immediate, intense demands were all-consuming. The actual transition moment from the Village to independent housing was the most vulnerable time for people who had lived unhoused for a very long time. The staff helped them as much as they could, but when they established housing and moved in, fear of uncertainty sometimes made people go back to their old lifestyle.

Andy observed that those most likely to succeed without regression or relapse were the residents who had taken advantage of the social networking offered by the Village. Those who stayed in contact with their social workers, their families, and support groups like Narcotics Anonymous, Alcoholics Anonymous, and the Healthy Moms program (a group for mothers in recovery), were the most likely to be successful.

Andy often worked closely with Betty as they served clients. He said, "If we think clients are lying or manipulating, we play good cop/bad cop. Betty is always the bad cop. She's really good at being a 'dragon mother.' She has high expectations and will push you until you are successful. She can be very motivating."

At the Village, one of the most striking sights are the pet dogs sitting at their owners' feet or rolling on their backs for a belly rub.

---

4 Betty Kwan Chinn Homeless Foundation website, https://www.bettychinn.org/, accessed January 2023.

This shelter was one of the few in the region to allow clients to bring their dogs, recognizing the importance of the security, attachment, and comfort they provided. For some people, their dog was their primary relationship, providing companionship and solace through otherwise long and lonely days. Particularly for some unsheltered women, a dog provided vital safety in a dangerous environment.

Local veterinarian Erzsi Willoughby provided free vaccinations, treatment, and medication for the dogs. Another donor paid licensing fees so all dogs were legal. In learning to be responsible pet owners, residents took a step toward shouldering other responsibilities as well. Noah Coleman was the Village case manager and in that role managed the grants that provided dog food, veterinarian care, flea medicine, dog crates, and all the rest of the pets' necessities. He acknowledged that the dogs provided an important companion for otherwise lonely people, and pointed out that it made it harder to find permanent rental housing when the time came.

There was a large open area at the Village covered with translucent roofing so it was protected and warm and sunny. This space became a place for eating, gathering, or simply sitting in the quiet and warmth. On one long wall was a mural painted by a church youth group who came to volunteer from Santa Rosa. These teenagers spent days with the residents of the Village and listened to their stories. Then they painted what they heard.

On the far left, the mural is dark with purple and black swirls. This is where many Village residents began, on the streets, in a dark place. Then a large sun appears. On its rays are painted the words, "Feed the hungry. Give drink to the thirsty. Clothe the naked. Shelter the homeless. Visit the imprisoned. Visit the sick. Bury the dead." A bridge stretches from the sun to a place of greenery and trees, a waterfall, flowers, and swirls of pink and yellow, representing a new beginning. Those who spent time in that peaceful space could project their own story onto the swirl of colors.

On Sundays, a group of several dozen college students from the Newman Center, a Catholic student club at Cal Poly Humboldt, came to work with Betty. At the Village, they gathered hygiene packets and sandwiches to distribute before heading out to the unhoused on the streets. Their assignment was simply to ask people if they wanted the supplies and food, and if they wanted someone to listen to them. Many students sat on sidewalks and listened to stories, whether factual or, for some, distorted due to mental illness. The students kept coming.

One woman came to the Village with two beloved pit bulls, but one of these dogs was aggressive and bit Betty twice. When the dog also bit two residents of the Village, it was time to call Animal Control. However, the man who had been most badly bitten refused and asked that the dog be given another chance. Fortuitously, a local professional dog trainer volunteered her services, offering three months of free training to the dog and her owner.

Under this tutelage, the dog settled down, became more responsive and less threatened (and therefore less threatening), and became a good resident of the Village. When the owner got a job and had to leave her dogs during the day, Betty fed them and developed her own relationship with the animals, an amazing feat given her early trauma with dogs. The client and her dogs were able to move to a local trailer park when a donor gave money for a small trailer. They lived there until the woman's final illness, when hospitalization became necessary.

For all the success stories of people who made it permanently off the streets, there were also those who were given a chance, started restoring their dignity and health, but then did not continue. Sometimes people failed out of Betty's programs by being unwilling or unable to stay off drugs or abide by the common rules.

This was difficult and heartbreaking each time it happened, but Betty did not give up. She continued to offer chances and hold hope that one day some seed of will and light would lead them out. And whenever it did, she would be there.

One such couple came to the Village with untreated mental illnesses and addiction, and their behavior was loud and aggressive. They had a baby with them, who was soon removed by Social Services. Not long after, Betty evicted them for aggressive non-compliance with the rules. It cost Betty $300 to clean up the damage they had done to the place they'd been given to stay.

After five more months on the street, the couple mutually decided they were at an end; they wanted to get clean. They entered a detox program, which they both successfully completed. By then the woman was pregnant again. They asked to come back. Betty knew that it might not work, but believing that everyone deserves a second chance, she asked the staff, and they were willing to take the risk. The couple did not want to lose another child and had decided to do whatever it took to remain a family.

Betty was not naive about the risk of regression or relapse for addicts whose minds and bodies have become dependent on a drug. But it is also true that a deeply held decision, a commitment from the depth of one's will, can sometimes be stronger. During her second stay in the Village, the mother was asked what advice she would give to other addicts wanting to recover. She replied, "You just have to decide for yourself, 'I'm done.' No one can do it for you. Even though life gets tough, and you want to numb it, it's better to stay with the present and cope with it. You have to learn acceptance of things in your life that you can't understand."

Sadly, this strong conviction was not enough to keep her and her partner from drugs, and they ended up back on the streets, which resulted in another child going into the system. Betty gives people a chance, supporting and guiding them as much as possible, but the rest is up to them. Some will succeed, and others will return to their former lives. Betty observed that for addicts who experience being clean, it can be powerful. That "clean up" moment, which some of those in Betty's care experienced before relapsing and returning to the streets, was enough for some to return and try sobriety once more. Betty never gave up on them.

Homeless Court was another vital service provided by Betty's work. She encouraged people on the streets to come to Betty's Blue Angel Village for an interview, to see if unresolved legal issues in their past could be cleaned up. Some agreed to turn themselves in to authorities to complete unfinished prison sentences. Others with minor crimes on the books were able to participate in Homeless Court. Often, the judge sentenced the offenders to community service, which they then discharged by working on community projects.

Once a person became unhoused, trying to survive and facing mental illness or addiction, as well as general debilitation, often prevented them from having the motivation or confidence to pursue solutions to the legal problems that kept them out of the workforce. Homeless Court was a step out of this quandary. Once their records were cleared, Betty helped them find employment.

One May day, Betty left her work to go to Humboldt State University (now Cal Poly Humboldt) for the commencement ceremony. She watched a young man walk across the stage, and she remembered when she first met him. He didn't have housing; his depression was so severe that he was on Supplemental Security Income (SSI) because of it. He had sunk under the weight of a minor legal problem he could not begin to know how to resolve. He had no family and no support network to call upon. Betty encouraged him, then accompanied him to Homeless Court.[5] Judge John Feeney gave him a chance to clear his record by performing twenty hours of community service, which he successfully completed. Once his legal record had been cleared, Betty helped him find a job doing yard work. He found out he had a talent for it, and earning money began to return to him a sense of agency. Betty next helped him find housing. As his depression improved and he gained self-esteem and confidence, he was eventually ready to go off of SSI and support himself. He decided to return to school.

Betty attended his graduation with the satisfaction of a mother. As with mothering, this was a long, step-by-step process, requiring endurance and persistence. The Village provided a resource-dense community that was able to aid in this process of restoration.

The Village gave residents access to all the services and resources of the main Day Center, including employment skills training, computer access, and medical and mental health services. But it also provided a community that, while temporary, could build relationships. For many people who spent a long time living unhoused, relationships were difficult to establish and maintain. Social skills for effective interaction may never have been acquired, or may have grown rusty from disuse.

---

5   Lisa Bethune, unpublished communications, 2007.

The defenses they had put up to survive on the street needed to be slowly disassembled. The Village gave people an opportunity to let go of old modes and begin again.

There were weekly community meetings and movie nights. Professionals provided free haircuts. There was a traveling library and laundry access. There was also a weekly community clean-up that allowed residents to give back to the community by cleaning up green spaces and roads. The goal at Betty's Blue Angel Village was that in three months, participants would be stable and equipped enough to move into an apartment.

Under the umbrella of the Betty Kwan Chinn Homeless Foundation, Betty now worked in four settings beyond her truck: the Betty Kwan Chinn Day Center, Betty's House Family Shelter, Betty's Blue Angel Village, and the Annex. The Annex, serving women and children, was housed in a large building across the street from the Day Center, refurbished in partnership with the city and St. Joseph Hospital. It housed women and their children who were subject to domestic violence and needed safe housing. During the COVID-19 pandemic, many families experienced increased stress and proximity resulting in more and more severe domestic violence. Betty opened the Annex to meet that need.

Betty in front of Betty's Annex

Supplemental Information

In 2015, Los Angeles declared a state of emergency due to homelessness. Mayor Eric Garcetti and Sofia Borges, director of the MADWORKSHOP Homeless Studio at the University of Southern California School of Architecture, were committed to finding ways to use housing design to expedite moving people from the streets to permanent housing. Word had traveled through California and beyond of the successful use of converted shipping containers as transitional housing for the houseless. Betty was invited to travel to L.A. to consult with Borges, her team, and Mayor Garcetti. In 2018, Borges and her co-editor R. Scott Mitchell, an assistant professor at the USC School of Architecture, published the results of their work in the book Give Me Shelter: Architecture Takes on the Homeless Crisis.[6]

Sofia Borges of the USC School of Architecture and Mayor Eric Garcetti stand with Betty in Los Angeles

---

6 R. Scott Mitchell and Sofia Borges, *Give Me Shelter: Architecture Takes on the Homeless Crisis* (San Francisco: ORO Editions, 2018).

Chapter 18

Hope from Sadness

"...no despair of ours can alter the reality of things; or stain the joy of the cosmic dance which is always there."

– Thomas Merton, *New Seeds of Contemplation*

Betty built deep and long-lasting relationships with her unhoused neighbors. Over the years, some became trusted friends and helpers. In 2006, she met James John James, who was called Jesse by his friends. Betty called him "my right-hand man." Betty trusted Jesse, and the two were friends united in a common cause of helping those living in the open. Always helpful and cheerful, he could be trusted to provide help and mentorship for young houseless people day or night. Jesse patiently mentored them.[1]

Betty was a mother figure to Jesse. At one point he needed a lot of dental work done, even preparing to pull his own teeth with pliers because of the pain. Betty found a local dentist who volunteered to help him. Betty went with him to the dentist and even went into the treatment room with him to ease his anxiety.

Jesse spent a lot of time at an encampment on the sand dunes near the Samoa Peninsula and served as a kind of agent for Betty among the unhoused there. She relied upon him. He was a liaison for Betty, calling her from his cell phone to let her know what resources were needed for particular people on any given day.

---

1 Lisa Bethune, unpublished communications, 2013.

On September 8, 2013, Jesse and his friend Mathew were hauling jugs of fresh water on their bikes back to the encampment when they encountered a twenty-one-year-old man and his sixteen-year-old girlfriend. This couple had recently traveled to Eureka from Clear Lake and were not known to the community at the encampment. Feeling afraid in their circumstances while looking for a safe place to camp, they had purchased crossbows the day before.

There was an encounter between the couple and Jesse and his friend. Insults were exchanged, which spiraled into a verbal fight. The couple shot both Jesse and Mathew with their crossbows. Mathew was hit several times and was seriously injured. Jesse was shot through the mouth and killed. Hours later, his dog Blackie was still by his side, guarding his body while the police investigated. Ultimately the male assailant took a plea deal and was sentenced to eighteen years in state prison.[2] The terrible irony is that Jesse, whom they killed, was the very person who would have taken them under his wing and helped them had he been given the chance.

Later, Betty received permission to scatter Jesse's ashes on the dunes where he had been killed.

~

Father Eric Freed arrived in Eureka in 2011 and served as the priest at St. Bernard Church. He had spent more than twenty years serving with his Salesian order as a high school teacher in Japan. He spoke and wrote fluently in Japanese, and loved the history, people, food, and culture of that land. While Japan and China are very different cultures, there was enough similarity for Betty to feel known and understood by Father Eric. They grew close. He was well loved by all, and was known to appreciate a fine Scotch, a good cigar, and lively conversation.

On New Year's Eve, 2013, Betty and Father Eric met to discuss his church's support of her charity. He gave her three large buckets of

---

2 Thadeus Greenson, "'A modern mountain man' Friends struggle to reconcile James James' violent end with the peaceful man they knew," *Eureka Times-Standard,* September 16, 2013.

Betty with supporter and friend Fr. Eric Freed (Photo by Gary Todoroff)

peanut butter for her feeding program. That was the last time Betty saw him. He lived in the rectory next to the church, and when he was late for the 9:00 a.m. Mass the next morning, a deacon went to look for him, and made the grisly discovery. In what appears to have been a random and deranged act, he was tortured, asphyxiated, and bludgeoned to death.

His assailant had been released from jail two hours before the assault, for he no longer met the legal criteria to be involuntarily held. He had been arrested the previous day when a citizen called 911 complaining of his wild and agitated behavior. He admitted to having taken heroin and methamphetamine. The jail was a short walk to the rectory.[3] A motive was never established. In April 2016, Father Eric's murderer was convicted on all charges.

When Father Eric's three sisters came to Eureka in April for the trial, they gave Betty a decorative plaque they thought their brother wanted her to have. It was a beautifully gilded wooden plaque with an indigo background on which were carved two Chinese characters. They could be translated as either "You Witness God's Love" or "You Speak Truth." She hung the plaque on the wall of her modest office at the Day Center as a reminder to be a witness to love and truth, no matter what.

For Betty, the incomprehensibility and senselessness of Jesse's and Father Eric's murders were all too reminiscent of the mistreatment and loss she endured during the Cultural Revolution. Now, decades later,

---

3 B.K. O'Neel, "Questions Remain in California Priest's Tragic Slaying," *The Catholic World Report*, January 16, 2014.

far across the world, for two different beloved people, evil had come. The darkness of which humans are capable is not limited to any one race, geography, political party, gender, class, or time. Betty's early loss came to her through governmentally orchestrated and systematic violence, while both Jesse's and Father Eric's deaths were a result of random, chaotic violence. Still, the effect was the same. Betty once again lost people whom she loved to a source outside of her control.

These losses remained a source of grief, sorrow, and pain for Betty. When she traveled near the site of Jesse's death on the sand dunes, she felt it in her body. But Betty did not give in to hopelessness, and chose to see beauty and light even when ugliness and darkness appeared. She had learned to hold the opposing forces, and to not be overwhelmed for long, when light seemed to have failed. She gathered herself from the deep well within her, and moved out to greet the next weary pilgrim on the road.

Chapter 19

Joy from Sadness

"Who we really are is the person revealed walking, like Shadrach in the fiery furnace, in the center of that moment when the pain meets and is illuminated by unconditional love."
– Dr. Cynthia Bourgeault, *Love is Stronger Than Death*

"How lucky is the soul that minds the heart!
For God, consoling the heart
that is broken into hundreds of pieces,
is better than going on pilgrimage.
God's treasures are buried in ruined hearts."
– Rumi

In 2018, after several years of relative quiet on the public stage, Betty was recognized as a CNN Hero. The CNN Heroes series was established to showcase "everyday people changing the world" and demonstrate the power of one person to do good.

This award, like the ones she had received before, highlighted Betty's desperate childhood circumstances and the transformation of her pain into service to the houseless.

Betty said when interviewed for the award, "The American people were so kind to me…when I came to the United States, it was the first time I experienced people smiling at me, and not knowing me. They just looked at me and smiled, and that stuck in my heart."[1]

---

1   Allie Torgan, "A horrific childhood in China inspires a crusade against homelessness," CNN Heroes, *CNN*, October 4, 2018.

Wendy, Betty's Sister, with their mother

For Betty to be smiled at by others had enormous power. Her own smile—vibrant, broad, and radiant—was in absolute opposition to her years of being disallowed eye contact. Being in America meant being free of the taint of the Devil Child label. Sadly, the past could not be so easily left behind.

When her sister Wendy was dying of cancer, Betty went to Washington State to take care of her for three months, fulfilling her promise to her dying father. Wendy was the last of the Kwan family to come to America. She had refused to leave their grandmother Ng, and emigrated from China only after her grandmother's death in 1980 and the ritual time of mourning.

Betty was utterly committed to Wendy, and the two were very close. After Wendy's emigration to the United States, she lived with Betty and Leung and their sons for eleven years, until she had saved enough money to buy her own house. Eventually Wendy married and moved to the Seattle area; she never had children. While Betty was caring for her dying sister, a person from their extended family blamed Betty for Wendy's illness because of Betty's reputation as a Devil Child. It was devastating for Betty. She thought she had moved far away from that label and safely into a new life. Now to have that accusation made once again, after decades, and while caring for her beloved dying sister, stirred intense feelings of shame, worthlessness, and abandonment.

Betty left the house immediately and went to the airport, where she sat for over a day waiting for a flight home. She no longer felt welcome in the community of the sister she had tried to help. This was crushing for Betty, on top of the wild grief of losing her sister soon after. For many years, Betty could not cry; she had learned to starve her emotions in the garbage dump. Only later would the tears come freely when she spoke of Wendy.

Even pain at such a deep level had not stopped Betty's relentless love. She seemed to meet each new obstacle by absorbing the pain and then converting it into more love.[2]

Jean and Tom

Jean and Tom came to Betty after losing their rental housing to a black mold infestation. Not having the requisite first and last month's deposit for a new rental, and owning two large dogs, they ended up on the street. Tom was a handyman, but his income was inconsistent and their extended family could only help for a short time. The couple bounced around from a motel to a handmade rock-and-wood structure behind the shopping mall, and finally to a tent. Jean was resourceful and found a way to make an orderly and clean abode, and even found a way to heat hauled water over a fire for bathing. Still, the behavior of the heroin addicts who lived near them made things difficult, and it was hard for them to find a job while living outdoors. It was hard to do much but simply survive.

Jean and Tom came to live at the Village, and then eventually, after another stint in a motel, to the apartment above the Day Center. By this time, Jean had become a staff member at the shower program and also an assistant cook to Betty. Tom had become the overnight support staff at the Village. Under Betty's mentorship, there was an enormous

---

2 In the fall of 1991, a young professor at a Washington state college lost his wife, mother, and daughter when their vehicle was hit by a drunk driver. He later wrote of that grief, "I didn't get over the loss of my loved ones; rather I absorbed the loss into my life, like soil receives decaying matter, until it became a part of who I am. Sorrow took up permanent residence in my soul and enlarged it." Similarly, Betty's soul has been enlarged by her pain as she has worked it into the center of her being.

change in their self-confidence, outlook, and hope. Jean simply affirmed, "Betty gave us a chance."

Jean and her husband now have a goal to buy a piece of property of their own. She said they just needed an opportunity to feel good about themselves, to work, and to prove themselves. Betty did that for them. Jean said, "Betty is an amazing woman. All the trials she's been through in her life and she keeps going all day, every day, nonstop. It's because she loves and cares about people. I love working with her. She's awesome!"

Jason

As a young child, Jason's birth mother left him with a male friend when she moved on. The friend married and his new wife did not want Jason. Neither of his birth parents could care for him, so he was sent to a long series of foster homes, sometimes a new one every week. He became afraid of close contact with people. He especially distrusted people who were too friendly to him because it reminded him of the first few days at a new foster home. The people were friendly when he arrived; they welcomed him and bought him things, but soon he'd be going to a new foster home. This revolving door of houses had taught him not to get attached and not to trust.

Painfully reserved, Jason came to Betty when he was eighteen years old. Like many former foster youth whom Betty helped, Jason had aged out of foster care and had nowhere to go. Betty was able to find a room in a friend's house for him. It was the first room of his own he'd ever had. Betty found Jason a part-time job, so he worked at the showers in the morning and went to his employment in the afternoon. Betty helped him replace the identification documents that had been destroyed with his camp during a police sweep. This was often a major impediment for the unhoused; without identification, there was no way to apply for any kind of services, work, or schooling. Betty then arranged help for him to enter the local community college, where he got a tuition grant. Jason suffered and struggled and experienced serious depression. There were no easy roads out of homelessness.

But Betty stuck by him and arranged a mental health evaluation for him, at which time he was diagnosed and began treatment for his emotional and developmental issues. To know that what he suffered had a name and was treatable was a huge step forward. When he regressed, Betty was there to encourage him. Slowly, haltingly, he made his way into independence and was employed, living on his own, and stable.

The Man from Yale

One day, a man came to Betty's attention who was quite different from the people she usually worked with. He was disoriented and did not know his birthdate, his full name, or his social security number. But he carried himself in a way that spoke of a former life that was different from the one he was now living. He had been unsheltered on the streets in many locations for a long time when Betty began to feed him. She noticed that he wore an old sweatshirt with a bulldog mascot printed on it. Since the local Fortuna High School had a similar mascot, she struck up a conversation with him, assuming he was from Fortuna. He corrected her, telling her he had attended Yale University. The confused man knew some of the street names on campus, and Betty recognized them from visiting her son who had graduated from there. Although the man recalled none of his other personal data, he somehow remembered his student I.D. number from Yale. On a hunch, Betty contacted an administrative office at Yale to find out if that number corresponded with a former student. It did. Thus identified, his family was contacted.

The man's former secretary, in what had been his successful business, ended up making an anonymous visit to observe him while Betty was serving him and others food. She confirmed his identity to his family, who then arranged for him to be evaluated by a physician. His family sent him a plane ticket, and Betty took him to the airport for the reunion.

They had not seen him in many years. He had simply disappeared one day in the aftermath of a divorce. His car had been found at a train station, but the trail then ran cold. In gratitude for the care Betty had provided and the sleuthing that led to his return to his family, they offered to support Betty's charity. Betty declined, asking them to instead donate to a charity near their home. Later, Betty received an acknowledgment from a nonprofit organization for the houseless on the East Coast, saying that the family had made a $10,000 donation in her name.

Ray

Ray was a very ill man with schizophrenia who had been living on the streets for about fifteen years. He slept on cardboard inside a recycling dumpster. He took the contents of his bed to the recycling center for odd bits of cash. Betty tried to get him into housing multiple times over the years. She spoke with him and offered him help. Ray did not appear interested. But he talked with Betty and looked forward to the donuts she brought.

One day, for reasons known only to him, Ray decided he was ready to take Betty up on her offer, and he came to the Village. For the first several weeks of his residence, the intensity of his hallucinations created some disturbing scenes. But with help from the staff and daily visits from a county mental health worker, Ray began to take his medication consistently, and his illness-induced phantasms receded. He became capable of interaction and reciprocal conversation, and therefore, of developing relationships.

For the first time in many years, Ray was housed, his physical and mental needs were cared for, and he was being restored to health. Ray came back to himself. His appearance was so changed—he was clean, groomed, and well-dressed—that he was not recognizable as the person who had lived on the streets. In addition to medication, manager Andy Pham believed that "listening to him and giving him a safe place to stay" were central to his improvement. Fifteen years is a long time to persist in offering help that is declined. Betty persisted.

Jared

Jared had a hard childhood, followed by struggles and losses as an adult that landed him on the streets. Betty began feeding him. One of the most powerful aspects of Betty's work with people like Jared was her intuitive ability to see beyond a person's appearance and circumstances to the core of their authentic self. She was astute and could accurately assess a person's readiness to be helped. Jared was ready. Her respect and love kindled a spark, long cold, of self-assurance and hope. Betty fanned that tiny spark into a fire by offering a shower, a meal, a temporary place to live, job training, employment opportunities, and, finally, help with finding an apartment. Her most powerful gift, though, was the simple belief that Jared was capable of making it.

Jared offered to help with the shower program and proved to be a reliable and conscientious worker. Soon he was helping Betty with many tasks throughout the day. She cared about him, and he enjoyed being useful.

When the Day Center was being built, he volunteered his time and was then hired on as crew. It turned out he had worked construction in the past and had some skills. When the Day Center project was complete, the construction foreman hired Jared and worked with him for several years until Jared himself became a foreman at another local construction firm. He credited it all to Betty's belief in him. He called it "the Betty Magic."

A gazebo arose on the grounds of the Day Center. It was elegantly made of beautiful redwood, with an inviting shape, like a harbor or

Gazebo built by Jared on the grounds of the Day Center

refuge. Chairs clustered within, an invitation for gathering. Jared built it for Betty. He said, "I wanted something that would represent what Betty did for me. As I built it piece by piece, I thought this must be how Betty felt when she was putting me back together."[3]

Young Woman

One day, Betty found a young woman lying in the bushes behind the Humboldt County Office of Education. The woman was hungry and asked Betty for food. She was wearing Liz Claiborne designer clothes and good leather shoes, and had expensive luggage. The disoriented woman was not sure how she had come to be in Eureka. Betty took her to a nearby motel, checked her in, told her to get some sleep, and said she would be back the next morning to check on her. Betty worried about the young woman's safety and told her not to leave the motel. Betty only had enough money remaining from a local church's offering to afford one more night in a motel for this woman.

The next morning, Betty asked the woman if she could call anyone on her behalf. She was able to give Betty several numbers, the closest of which was in Portland, Oregon. Betty called and explained who she was. The woman answering the phone thought Betty was soliciting money for a nonprofit, until she heard her friend's name, a former high school companion. Betty handed over her phone, and the two old friends talked for a long time.

The Portland friend told Betty they had been looking for the missing woman for quite some time. Her friend arranged for a nicer hotel and sent the woman a ticket for a flight to Oregon. Six or seven months later, Betty received a call from Ohio, from a college friend of the same woman. That friend explained to Betty that the woman had had a mental collapse after a broken relationship. She had begun to shop compulsively, and at the same time lost her job. As the debts mounted, her house in southern California was foreclosed on, her cars

---

3   Lisa Bethune, unpublished communications, 2019.

were repossessed, and she had left with only some clothes and her suitcase.

Her ties to reality became frayed and she ended up in a mental hospital. Having no family to call upon, when she was discharged the hospital officials put her on a Greyhound bus, letting her choose whether to travel north or south. She chose north and ended up at the last California bus stop, on Fourth Street in Eureka. Betty found her not long afterward. During the phone call half a year later, the Ohio friend reported that this woman was now living with her in a farming community and was getting help.

Several years later, Betty unexpectedly received a Christmas card from the woman she had found in the bushes. It contained good news: she was working as an accountant for a nonprofit, she no longer compulsively shopped, and her mental illness was well managed. She told Betty she was doing well.

Betty was so effective because she knew the stories of almost every person, and the smile and hug she always offered were as important to the heart as the food she provided was to the body. However, she also knew how to speak up when needed. When several men were sitting on the sidewalk smoking marijuana outside the Annex, Betty walked over to them and told them to leave. They did so. When a client was rude to a staff member, Betty intervened with resolute authority. If a client did not modify their behavior, they were shown the door.

Chapter 20

The Dance Goes On

"Yet the fact remains that we are invited to forget ourselves on purpose, cast our awful solemnity to the winds and join in the general dance."

– Thomas Merton, *New Seeds of Contemplation*

Betty made phone calls as she walked, solving problems and making decisions as needs arose throughout her day. She worked ceaselessly from before dawn to after dark. It could be a staff member calling about a disruptive resident who had again broken the rules; the regretful decision was made to evict. A new mother could be having trouble sleeping because of her crying infant; staff in the Family Shelter were asked to provide the mother breaks. Someone needed medical care; they received an immediate referral to the clinic. Someone could not drive to work because their car was broken; arrangements were made to get it fixed. And in the midst of it all, Betty was cooking, transporting, and delivering meals, going to board meetings and local government meetings, addressing community groups, and engaging with her staff. These selfless everyday acts flowed in a constant stream. She seemed not to notice.

One day Betty showed up late for a meeting. It was a bitterly cold November day. She was damp and dressed in inadequate, light cotton pants, and offhandedly explained that she had given her warm sweats to one of the women she feeds because the woman was wet and cold.

California Polytechnic University, Humboldt President Tom Jackson presenting Betty with an Honorary Doctorate of Humane Letters

She said the woman had an infected spider bite on her leg and could not afford antibiotics, so Betty was on her way to get medicine as soon as the meeting ended. When she gave the woman her sweats, all she had in her truck was an old pair of thin pants.

Betty was in constant motion and yet seemed still and quiet at her core. Unless you happened to follow her for a day, you would not know the incredible volume of help that flowed from one small woman. The network of goodwill and trust that she established in the community was truly amazing. Help getting a bus ticket, a hotel room, or even a vehicle was a phone call away. Those with financial resources had learned to trust that Betty distributed those resources with wisdom and efficiency. Betty was a middle person between people in the community (and beyond) who wanted to give and those who needed it most. Because of her deep relationships with both the givers and the receivers, the exchange was made in the most effective, targeted, and useful way possible.

Because Betty never took anything for herself, and not even appreciation or acclaim were of much interest to her, there was a sense of untainted wholesomeness in her work that resonated with all involved. She was once told by her business manager that there were no funds to buy food for nine days until some promised funding came in. Betty responded, "I have fully committed myself to God so I am not going to worry; I am going to trust Him." Within several hours, without anyone else having been told, a completely unexpected donation for $1,000 arrived at the center. The next day, an even larger, unsolicited donation was received.[1] That kind of remarkable event happened regularly. While Betty was delighted, it did not seem to surprise her at all.

After four decades of this work in Humboldt County, Betty rarely goes anywhere without seeing someone whom she has helped. On a day when Humboldt County was requiring all front-line workers to be tested for COVID-19, Betty and eleven of her staff were tested. One of the medical technicians performing the procedure for the long line of workers was in tears when she saw Betty. Betty looked closely and realized that this woman was someone with whom she had once walked the healing road. Betty had arranged tuition for the training that now allowed this skilled technician to perform the tests. This was Betty's everyday experience.

In the spring of 2022, Betty received an Honorary Doctorate of Humane Letters from California Polytechnic University, Humboldt, one of only thirteen awarded in the university's 109-year history.

This award had profound meaning for Betty because of her lost opportunity for education. She often covered her embarrassment about her literacy deficits by saying, "I don't do paperwork," but the sting of never having been able to attend school never abated. This award was "like pulling a thorn out of her skin." Betty felt this award "is for my work, and also personal … it really gets into my heart and soul."[2] With this honorary doctorate, things had come full circle. In her acceptance speech, she spoke of the boy she took to school from the marsh who became a doctor. She spoke of her awe that this boy whom she had helped was now saving lives.

Betty arrived at the person she is today by a long and difficult road. Along the way, she has suffered. She has forgiven. She has suffered again. She has forgiven again. And throughout the journey, her very

---

1 Private conversation between Betty and the author on July 1, 2020.
2 Ryan Burns, "Beloved Local Activist Betty Chinn to Receive Honorary Doctorate from Cal Poly Humboldt," *Lost Coast Outpost*, February 16, 2022.

being was stamped by humility, integrity, and joy. Somehow, in the crucible of her anguish, Betty came to forgiveness rather than to hostility and resentment. She herself seemed surprised by this fact. It is a mystery why suffering can lead to brokenness and lasting despair in some and perseverance and hope in others.

Betty does not try to be someone else. By renouncing everything but loving service she has found herself. She did not even know she was following the spiritual pattern of losing her life to find it.[3] Betty was doing what made her whole. She does not strive for praise, power, or wealth; they hold no interest for her. She is continually surprised by the attention she receives and the awards that have come her way. "How did this happen?" she asks with genuine puzzlement. She credits the Divine; "How could anyone see my life and not know it is God?" The paradox is that her complete lack of self-interest and her complete self-giving have become a powerful message—one she never set out to send, but which in its authenticity and rarity has touched many people.

Betty followed the path of descent into the worst humanity can do to each other. And she traveled the path of ascent to a place of transformative forgiveness and love. She became fully alive. In living her life in the service of others, she became free. She was not a servant to anything but the mandate of love as she understood it in any given moment. She took into her heart the "other" so totally that the distinction between her own self, her own needs, and those whom she served ceased to be meaningful. She was a part of them, and she invited them to become a part of her, in the circle of love in which all things hold together. Within this circle, there was joy. Betty radiated delight in triumphs large and small: in people taking tiny steps toward health and independence, or in another gray bird singing in her garden at home. The dance of self-forgetting, which produced joy, became so habitual that it seemed likely to continue each day of her life. Betty had never known her actual birthdate, though she "chose" September 13 as a guess based on the Chinese calendar. She said, "Every day I can get up, that is my birthday."

---

3 Jesus in Matthew 16:25 and Mark 8:34.

" 'Come, you who are blessed by my Father, inherit the kingdom prepared for you from the foundation of the world, for I was hungry and you gave me food, I was thirsty and you gave me something to drink, I was a stranger and you welcomed me, I was naked and you gave me clothing, I was sick and you took care of me, I was in prison and you visited me.' Then the righteous will answer him, 'Lord, when was it that we saw you hungry and gave you food or thirsty and gave you something to drink? And when was it that we saw you a stranger and welcomed you or naked and gave you clothing? And when was it that we saw you sick or in prison and visited you?' And the king will answer them, 'Truly I tell you, just as you did it to one of the least of these brothers and sisters of mine, you did it to me.' "
– Jesus, in Matthew 25: 34-41

Betty was traumatized beyond the ability of a young body and mind to endure; there were repercussions. That she survived at all is a feat of resilience, courage, and strength.

In 2002, Kaiser Permanente published a pivotal study in collaboration with the Centers for Disease Control and Prevention.[1] The results were astounding and have greatly expanded our understanding of the far-reaching effects of childhood neglect and abuse on adult mental and physical health. Studies have confirmed the direct effect of cumulative adverse childhood experiences (ACEs), as they are known, on a wide range of psychological and physical problems.[2]

Betty's experience is something far beyond what the screening devices were designed to measure. There is no box to check for chronic torture.

As a little girl, Betty endured the full panoply of tortures commonly employed during the Cultural Revolution. Her family home was raided and possessions confiscated or destroyed. She was beaten, humiliated, "struggled against" by crowds, and made to wear a condemning wooden sign around her neck. Her family was separated, her mother imprisoned, and her siblings sent to labor camps. She and her siblings were denied an education and made "political orphans." Among other cruelties, she suffered starvation, exposure, neglect, and deprivation. She was made to eat the inedible and to chew rocks until her teeth broke. She suffered the death of her baby sister in her arms and was made to witness the execution of her eldest brother and his wife. She watched the bludgeoning to death of her infant brother, who was also cannibalized. She was made to watch multiple tortures of her mother,

---

1   Vincent J. Felitti, M.D., "The Relation Between Adverse Childhood Experiences and Adult Health: Turning Gold into Lead," *The Permanente Journal* 6, no. 1 (2002): 44–47.
2   Among them are depression, suicide, smoking, substance abuse, obesity, hypertension, diabetes, heart disease, and multiple other health outcomes.

including branding and bludgeoning. Betty was forced to kneel on broken glass, haul water for many hours a day in a labor camp, and endure live burial, near drowning, scalding, and choking. She was not allowed to speak or make eye contact.

When these stories were first told to the author, Betty had no idea that there was a growing body of literature that echoed, confirmed, and validated her memories. Now that writings like those cited here are available to Betty, they serve as a larger context for her own experience.

Unsurprisingly, Betty has suffered virtually all of the symptoms of post-traumatic stress disorder (PTSD) over the years. Diagnostically, she at one time fit every criterion. She has worked with several excellent therapists in the past who helped her in her recovery and to whom she is deeply grateful. She also had faithful family and friends; one couple in particular walked the long healing journey with her every step of the way.

Betty has an unusual internal resilience that is beyond what most in her position could call upon. Even when suffering from severe flashbacks, intrusive body memories, and other symptoms, she carried on with raising her children and her life's work of feeding the houseless. This work has been her lodestar, the compass bearing that has directed most of her life for the past forty years.

Our brains have evolved to scan for danger; this protective bias works to keep us safe. Within the limbic system, various structures, including the amygdala and hypothalamus, activate the sympathetic nervous system, which is then primed to set off the freeze, flight, or fight reaction. In the face of danger, the most primitive level of the brain takes over. Adrenaline and cortisol, among other hormones and neurotransmitters, are emitted to prepare the body for running or fighting or freezing. When Betty was made to sit still and quiet in the garbage dump, or forced into the well for hour upon hour, or pushed into a hole with dirt poured over her, her nervous system helped her to freeze, to go numb and still, in the service of her survival. When she could not bear what was being done to her, dissociation numbed and fogged her experience into a distant haze, again in the service of survival. The memories laid down during trauma are affected by these conditions. "…[M]emories are not formed and then pristinely maintained…Rather, memories are formed and then rebuilt anew every time they are accessed, i.e. remembered."[3]

When she was fleeing with her siblings, for many months her nervous system likewise emitted enormous amounts of stress hormones, in this case to activate movement and allow the body to keep going long beyond what exhaustion, thirst, and hunger would normally permit. But these neurological accommodations in the face of danger do not come without a price. Experiences sculpt the brain of a growing child. The brain forms familiar and habituated neural pathways that unconsciously determine reactions and experiences. "Neurons that fire together wire together."[4] That is, things experienced and held in the mind and body at the same time tend to fuse into an associational network. This fact explains why, for a person with PTSD, a certain smell, sound, or sight can trigger a physiological reaction that appears unrelated to present circumstances. It is the past intruding on the present.

For many years, Betty could not eat anything barbecued because the smell made her feel nauseated. Eventually she made the connection between the smell of her mother's branded flesh and her revulsion at the smell of barbecue. A similar neural association caused her to feel intense aversion to the smell of gasoline; she could not fill her own car with gas. She realized that the smell of the gasoline thrown on a boy who was immolated was an associational trigger. When at a gas station smelling fuel, her body implicitly remembered the burning boy and reacted accordingly.

It was decades after Betty's escape before she could comfortably eat uncooked food. Fresh salad and vegetables were unpalatable. Again, she eventually realized that they reminded her of the insects, leaves, and snakes she had to eat to survive.

Over the years, Betty experienced frequent episodes of full-on flashbacks, including implicit, somatic memory: the memory that comes as an impression, a somatic sensation, or an intense emotion

---

3 Peter A. Levine, *Trauma and Memory: Brain and Body in a Search for the Living Past: A Practical Guide for Understanding and Working with Traumatic Memory* (Berkeley: North Atlantic Books, 2015), 140.
4 Ibid., 138.

but is not connected to a clear cognitive grasp of the actual event. The process of healing has included learning to recognize what is happening when implicit memories of trauma are triggered, and knowing how to self-soothe.

As she recognized the old patterns, Betty moved into new patterns of positive thought and action that allowed her nervous system to reestablish equilibrium. Only by tremendous acts of will and courage has Betty been able to develop new neural pathways that she can use to calm and settle her reactive nervous system. These inner strengths were overwhelmed at the time the trauma occurred. In the process of learning to maintain calm and clarity in the face of awful memories, they could be reconsolidated and "accessed, embodied, reinvigorated, and allowed to fully complete and express themselves."[5]

Trauma researcher Peter A. Levine describes the root of trauma as being accumulated energy from heightened arousal that has never been fully discharged.[6] He says that properly discharging those energies is key to healing. As Betty so often says, her passion for her work has in fact been part of her healing. It has allowed her meaningful, constructive opportunities to discharge energies that otherwise might have found more symptomatic expression. Dr. Levine, in working with those who have healed their trauma, says the wounded need to be willing to let go of their attachment to their symptoms and must have the desire to heal. Betty had that desire to let go and move on from the marks of her trauma. Levine also says of those he has seen heal, "I must confess that the miracles of healing I have seen make some higher form of wisdom and order hard to deny. Perhaps a better way of putting it is that there is an innate natural wisdom whose laws provide order in the universe. How can such a thing happen if there is no god, no wisdom, no tiger in the universe?"[7]

What Betty often says of her calling has become her motto: "It is not my work; it is my passion." She believes, and often states, that her life of pouring herself out for the needy and houseless has healed her

---

5 Ibid., 142.
6 Peter A. Levine, *Waking the Tiger: Healing Trauma* (Berkeley: North Atlantic Books, 1997), 37.
7 Ibid., 219.

own heart. Interestingly, this is biologically likely. It is not reliving trauma that seems to best heal it, but rather discharging the stored energy of the trauma held in the mind and body. Professional therapy has been an important and essential tool for Betty in this process. And the constant, daily discharge of physical and emotional energy into doing what gives her meaning and joy has been a continuous component of her healing.

Levine says, "Held within the symptoms of trauma are the very energies, potentials, and resources necessary for their constructive transformation."[8] Betty has tapped those energies and potentials daily for decades, and in so doing has used the path of suffering to grow into wholeness. It is not a wholeness free of suffering or difficulty—rather it is a wholeness of spirit that has learned to work alongside those issues and continue onward on the force of love.

Betty has used the energy of her own wounding to help others, and in so doing has helped heal herself. Her PTSD symptoms have greatly improved over the years, although sometimes a trigger will cause a resurgence. She knows that she might endure these moments for the rest of her life.

Any reader who may suffer from PTSD, or has been triggered by the events described in this book, is strongly encouraged to seek the professional help of a therapist trained in working with trauma. Professional societies of therapists trained in Somatic Experiencing and in Eye Movement Desensitization and Reprocessing (EMDR) can be reached at the sites below.

EMDR International Association

Email: info@emdria.org
Mailing Address: 7000 N Mo Pac Expy, Suite 200, Austin, TX. 78731-3013
Phone: 512-451-5200

Somatic Experiencing International

Email: traumahealing.org
Mailing Address: PO Box 7240, 8800 W. 116th Circle,
    Broomfield, CO. 80021
Phone: 303-652-4035

---

8 Ibid., 37.

Leung Chinn

Leung Chinn's family background is rich with the historical detail that defines the early beginnings of many Chinese Americans.[1] His first eight years were spent in his home village, in the same Guangdong Province where Betty's family came from, but with starkly different circumstances. His family was poor, living in a small home without electricity or toilet facilities and without physical comforts of any kind. Leung's family was like those to whom the Kwan family gave food.

Leung's grandfather, who was born with the surname Louie, immigrated to America before the Great Depression. He was forced to leave Guangdong Province due to a lack of jobs and abysmal poverty. He gained legal immigrant status in the U.S., but because of the Chinese Exclusion Act of 1882, there was no path to naturalization or citizenship for those without elite status. The Chinese Exclusion Act was finally repealed in 1943.

Leung's grandfather lived apart from his wife and children for

---

1 The story of Leung Chinn's family and life are largely derived from several interviews with the author in May 2020.

decades, working and sending money home. Because he was not a citizen, his family was not allowed to join him. However, the great fire that destroyed much of San Francisco after the earthquake in 1906 opened a method of bypassing this citizenship problem. Since most public records were destroyed in the fire, Chinese immigrants and others could claim that they had been born in America and thus were citizens. They bought records to document this; brokers and middlemen facilitated the transactions. A family named Chin, who claimed many offspring, had documents to sell. Leung's grandfather procured one, enabling him to claim citizenship for his son, Ark. This allowed Leung's grandfather to bring Ark to America. Now the Louies became Chins (and, eventually, Chinns). These "paper sons" were very common among the forebears of Chinese American families, though many of their children never learned of it.[2]

Leung's father, Ark, took the opportunity provided by his "paper son" status to join his father in America, in hopes that he might provide a better life for his family—including his wife, who was pregnant with Leung. Leung did not meet his father until he was eight years old.

When Leung was born, his mother gave him the first name of "Thank," which appears on his immigration papers. His grandmother gave him the name "Leung," which he adopted. There were virtually no young men or women in his village; they had all left grinding poverty to find jobs elsewhere, including Canada, the U.S., and southeastern Asia. Leung knew that young girls were sent off to become servants and had heard of infants who could not be fed and were left out in baskets "like Moses."[3]

Leung's mother, aunt, and grandmother lived off the rice they grew on their tiny plot of land and any money his father and grandfather could send home.

Ark completed his route to naturalization by serving in the U.S. Navy during World War II. He was then able to bring Leung and his

---

2 Hansi Lo Wang, "Chinese-American Descendants Uncover Forged Family Histories," *Morning Edition*, NPR, December 17, 2013, https://www.npr.org/sections/codeswitch/2013/12/17/251833652/chinese-american-descendants-uncover-forged-family-history.

3 This was common practice in rural China (Mungello, *Drowning Girls in China*, 10).

mother to San Francisco on a Navy transport ship in 1947. The first time Leung ever saw an automobile was on this trip.

Leung's uncle, Ark's older brother, had been a pilot in the famous Flying Tigers. His plane was shot down in the Second Sino-Japanese War, which left Ark responsible for his brother's family; he became a father to his nephew, who also came with them to America. The family spent about ten days quarantined at Angel Island Immigration Station in San Francisco Bay before moving to Seattle, where Leung's grandfather had established a small hand laundry. Leung and his family were in America before the Cultural Revolution began in China.

Leung was placed in the first grade when he started school in Seattle. He spoke no English and could not yet read or write. By the end of his first year of schooling, he had been moved up to the third grade, and by the fifth grade, he was competing in, and winning, county-wide history contests. He was clearly intelligent. Leung recalled some harassment in the fifth grade, when he was one of only four non-white students. He is not sure if the bullying was because he was Chinese or because he was the teacher's pet.

Leung worked in the strawberry fields and in his grandfather's laundry to earn money. He learned math by tallying his grandfather's receipts on an abacus. His father opened a small grocery store and a ten-cent store; Leung worked in the grocery store and later the ten-cent store every day after school, every weekend, and all summer until he started college. In high school, his physics teacher recognized that he was exceptional. This teacher brought a calculus book to school for Leung, which he worked through on his own, problem by problem. He was especially entranced by physics. While working for his father, Leung said, "I would do math and physics problems in my head while I stocked the shelves." He received an A in every class he took from eighth grade through twelfth grade with one exception, which was a B+ in his high school world history class.

He received a full scholarship from Texaco to the University of Washington. Because he tested out of calculus his freshman year, he had extra units, which he filled with classes in philosophy, religion, and psychology. He did well enough at university to receive another full scholarship and a research assistantship for his Ph.D. However, Leung says he never really felt he worked that hard. He had seen the incredible effort his grandfather and father had expended to give their family a foothold in America. Leung also witnessed racism against both his grandfather, in his laundry, and his father, in his grocery store. He was well aware of the scapegoating that could emerge against the "other," though in a very different context than Betty later experienced it.

Leung was bothered by chronic fatigue and weakness throughout his life. Only before a surgery at age seventy-eight was he diagnosed with alpha thalassemia, an inherited blood disorder that results in anemia. He accomplished a great deal in the face of an undiagnosed chronic health condition and an impoverished early life.

In spite of the courage, discipline, and intellectual strength implicit in his story, Leung is self-effacing and modest. He says, over and over, "I was the lucky one. I was lucky or God was watching out for me." It requires grace for him to say this, for his father's life was cut tragically short. A robber with a pistol murdered Ark in his ten-cent store while stealing beer. Leung was only twenty-two years old when he stepped into the role as head of his family. From then on, he cared for his grandmother, his mother, and his two much younger brothers. He shouldered the heavy responsibility and completed a Ph.D. in physics while doing so.

Lawrence and Stuart Chinn

Lawrence, Leung, Betty, and Stuart at the White House

When Betty was awarded the Presidential Citizens Medal in 2010, it was illuminating for her sons, Lawrence and Stuart Chinn. Because her work expanded significantly after they left home, and she did not talk about it, they were surprised to learn about all she had accomplished and discover how widely her reputation had spread. While Lawrence and Stuart both spoke proudly and lovingly of their mother, it was clear that neither one understood the scope of her activities before she was recognized by President Obama.

Stuart described his mother as a genuine and energetic person who expressed her feelings openly and was extremely loving throughout his childhood. He shared a particularly deep insight into one aspect of his mother: He recognized that she felt inadequate about her lack of formal education. His father, his brother, and he were all highly educated,[1] and he knew his mother suffered for having been denied that opportunity. However, he saw that in her charity work, she was doing something neither he nor his father or brother could ever do. Her trauma and loss equipped her to serve in ways they could not.

Subsequently, Betty's sons became actively involved in their mother's work. They have both been financially and morally supportive of her charitable endeavors.

Like Stuart, Lawrence was astonished by the award his mother received from President Obama. He described his mother as hardworking, modest, and unassuming, and said she had never told them the extent of her charity work. He knew her as a parent who, along with their father, prioritized her children. His father taught him to solve problems in his nightly homework, while his mother patiently played with both boys and was always involved in their schooling and activities. Lawrence said, "For us growing up, their only expectation was that we at least try. They weren't as focused on the results as on the process."

Finding out that she managed a huge charity—going on for years before they left home—surprised him greatly.

Lawrence, like Stuart, expressed deep appreciation and respect for both of his parents. He said of them, "They are patient, unassuming, and genuine."

Both sons recognized the vast store of family knowledge their mother held in her memory. She recalled every relative from both sides of the family, where they lived, how to contact them, and how they're related, whether by blood or by marriage. This archival memory was characteristic of Betty and exhibited itself in her daily work; she retained reams of knowledge about the history of clients past and present. She

---

1 Lawrence attended the University of California at Davis and earned a degree in biochemistry. He has spent nearly twenty years in the biotech industry as a medical researcher working on cancer treatments. He is married to Amy, an accountant, with whom he shares a son, Benjamin. Stuart attended Yale University for ten years, earning his B.A., Ph.D., and J.D. He is a tenured professor of law and an associate dean of the law school at the University of Oregon.

also remembered the names and stories of virtually every child who ever attended Lafayette Elementary School in the years she worked there.

Lawrence noted that staying connected with family on both sides was important to his parents. As a family, they spent significant amounts of time traveling to visit extended family members. He said that his mother would give them "mini-refresher courses" on the proper protocol and forms of address for each relative. It was only after he had gone away to college that he realized that it was not necessarily the norm for people to expend so much time and energy to nurture family connections. Lawrence shared a sweet memory of his patient mother making dim sum, a traditional Cantonese meal of small, bite-sized portions served with tea. The proper ingredients were not available in Eureka, so Betty made everything from scratch. Her boys wanted to "help," and Betty would give them bits of the dough, add food coloring, and let them use it like Play-Doh.

Lawrence also spoke of how incredibly hard-working his parents were. "It's in their DNA," he said. In the warmth both sons expressed toward their parents, it is clear that they were deeply, thoroughly nurtured. Betty and Leung gave to them all that Betty longed for but was denied by the Cultural Revolution.

Betty's sons are a living testament to her decision not to give in to despair on the day the gray bird sang.

HOPE IS MORE THAN
PLAYFUL IMAGINATION!
I COULDN'T IMAGINE IF HOPE DIDN'T EXIST
HOPE CAN TURN A POOR SOUL RICH
I KEEP HOPE ON MY BUCKET LIST
AS LONG AS HOPE IS ALIVE
IT'LL SERVE AS THE FUEL TO MY DRIVE
HOPE IS WHY MOST STRIVE
HOPE MAKES DOUBT HIDE

HOPE IS HIP!
ALWAYS IN STYLE
HOPE IS LIKE A ROPE
WHEN YOU'RE IN A DARK HOLE
AND NEED IT THE MOST

HOPE CAN MAKE THE HOPELESS GLOW!
HOPE CAN TURN A ROOKIE INTO A PRO
HOPE IS NOT A HOAX
HOPE IS LIKE A HOME
HOPE IS LIKE A BEAUTIFUL POEM

HOPE IS STILL THERE
WHEN ALL ELSE IS GONE.
I KEEP HOPE IN MY POCKET
FEELING LIKE I JUST WON THE LOTTERY!
BUT JUST A LITTLE HOPE...
CAN KEEP THE HEART FROM HARDENING.

-Rashad Hedgepeth

In mid-2023 a series of large, colorful murals were commissioned to be painted by various artists throughout the city of Eureka. Betty very much wanted a mural on her Day Center wall, and was talking with an artist about doing the project, but found out that the city grant covering artist's fees did not extend to the location of the Day Center.

At the same time, a woman came to visit Humboldt with her high-school-aged daughter, looking at colleges. This woman was the little girl who at age seven had approached Betty at Lafayette School to say: "Mrs. Chinn I am hungry". This was the child whose plea had launched Betty's life work. Now a successful businesswoman and mother, this person offered to pay for the painting of the mural on Betty's Day Center wall. The mural itself, without consultation from Betty, is aptly emblematic of Betty's life and her emergence into hope and light. The artist, Mir de Silva, even depicted a bird in flight.

Clergy participate in groundbreaking for the showers. L to R: Michael Tully (former president of St. Vincent de paul), Rev. David Samelson, Betty Chinn, Rev. Dan Price, Rev. Paul Harris

City officials participate in ground breaking for the showers. L to R: former City Councilman Larry Glass, Betty Chinn, former Eureka Mayor Virginia Bass, former police chief Garr Nielson

Betty serving as the Grand Marshall at the local Rhododendron Parade

First woman Supreme Court Justice Sandra Day O'Connor, who receieved the 2010 Minerva Award, here with Betty at the ceremony

Betty speaking at the College of the Redwoods Commencement Ceremony in 2009

U.S. Congressman Jared Huffman presents award to Betty at Day Center opening.
(Photo by Gary Todoroff)

The Ignation Faith Sharing Group which follows the spiritual exercises of St. Ignatius.
L to R front row: Rafael Cuevas, Claire Camozzi, Betty Chinn, Sue Rydz, Rick Graey
L to R back row: Liz McGee, Linda Bareilles, Amie Ricke, Ann Lynch, Fr. Bernard D'Sa

Lifetime friend, supporter and chronicler of Betty's stories, Lisa Bethune

Betty with former Eureka Police Chief Garr Nielson, who became a strong supporter

Betty with spiritual mentors Fr. Bob Benjamin and Ann Lynch

Kurt and Kim Kramer, construction company owners and supporters of Betty, join Betty at the blessing of the new storage containers which became Betty's Blue Village.

Betty and Judge John Feeney outside of her communiy shower. Judge Feeney presided over the Homeless Court for many years.

Early portrait of Betty

The 100th birthday celebration of Betty's mother in 2007

In Chinese culture, it is important not to die barefoot. When Betty found a pair of shoes similar to those her grandmother wore upon her death, she bought them. They are a continual reminder to Betty that, "you can not take my soul, no matter what you do to me."

Brother Alex's wedding reception in San Francisco. L to R: Wendy, Kathy, Faye, Lin (King's wife), Helen (cousin), Pat, Betty

Betty and family at son Lawrence's wedding wearing traditional Chinese wedding atire

Betty and family at son Lawrence's wedding wearing traditional American wedding atire

Betty amd Noah Coleman, the Case Manager Supervisor, outside Blue Angel Village

Maria Shriver and Betty in front of Betty's Blue Angel truck. (Photo by Gary Todoroff)

St. Francis

Like St. Francis, Betty was born into wealth, suffered greatly in imprisonment, and transformed that pain, giving herself to service to the poor.

St. Francis of Assisi was born in 1182 to a wealthy merchant family. As was common, he had a fear of and disgust for lepers, who represented as many as one in thirty people at that time. In the Middle Ages, it was falsely thought that leprosy was highly contagious, and some saw it as punishment for sin.

Young Francis was called "the King of Revels," given to partying, and he had lofty ideas of becoming a knight. However, his first foray into battle resulted in his capture and almost year-long imprisonment. He suffered serious illness and deep disillusionment. When he was released from prison, he was a changed man.

Francis saw a leper on the road, and quelling his revulsion and instinct to turn aside, he instead got off his horse, took the man in his arms, and kissed him. He wrote: "When I had once become acquainted with them, what had previously nauseated me became a source of physical consolation to me."[1]

The suffering that Francis endured broke down barriers between self and other. He no longer saw himself as separate from the poor or the ill. He learned the humility of solidarity and no longer approached the world in a hierarchical way. He began to see the divine in everyone and in everything.

Francis went on to minister at the leper hospitals and serve the poor as a barefoot itinerant. His complete self-surrender, ironically, led to influence. He spoke with popes, sultans, and, daily, the poor who were his brothers and sisters.

Lepers were still plentiful in the 1960s in Guangdong Province

---

1 The Testament of St. Francis

in China. Betty's mother was treating lepers who were subject to superstitious avoidance and victim-blaming, much as they had been during St. Francis's time. Betty's mother took care of them and advocated for them. And then her daughter, Betty, after her own imprisonment and suffering, in a sort of spiritual lineage, took up the cause of the poor, the abandoned, the addicted, the mentally ill, and the unhoused. She walks with them daily, letting her actions speak for her.

The prayer of St. Francis describes people like Betty well:

Lord, make me an instrument of your peace:
where there is hatred, let me sow love;
where there is injury, pardon;
where there is doubt, faith;
where there is despair, hope;
where there is darkness, light;
where there is sadness, joy.
O divine Master, grant that I may not so much seek
to be consoled as to console,
to be understood as to understand,
to be loved as to love.
For it is in giving that we receive,
it is in pardoning that we are pardoned,
and it is in dying that we are born to eternal life.

Bibliography

Abraham, Terry, and Priscilla Wegars. "Urns, Bones and Burners: Overseas Chinese Cemeteries." *Australasian Historical Archaeology* 21 (2003): 58–69. http://www.jstor.org/stable/29544506.

Bethune, Lisa. Unpublished communications. 2007, 2010, 2013, 2014, 2016, 2019, 2020.

————. Fundraiser speech at "An Evening with Betty" event at the Day Center. May 15, 2015.

"Betty Chinn awarded log-awaited letter from Mr. McFeely of 'Mr. Roger's Neighborhood.'" *Eureka Reporter*. September 20, 2008.

Bono, *Surrender, 40 Songs, One Story*. New York: Alfred A. Knopf, 2022.

Burns, Ryan. "Beloved Local Activist Betty Chinn to Receive Honorary Doctorate from Cal Poly Humboldt." *Lost Coast Outpost*. February 16, 2022. https://lostcoastoutpost.com/2022/feb/16/beloved-local-activist-betty-chinn-receive-honorar/.

Camus, Albert. "Return to Tipasa." In *Lyrical and Critical Essays* edited by Philip Thody. New York: Vintage Books, 1970.

Cheek, Timothy. *Mao Zedong and China's Revolutions: A Brief History with Documents*. Boston: Bedford/St. Martins, 2002.

Chen, Bing'an. *The Great Escape to Hong Kong*. United States: American Academic Press, 2019.

Chen, Laurie and Yujing Liu. "Explainer: how Hong Kong has for decades been a magnet for refugees and migrants." *South China Morning Post*. December 23, 2017. https://www.scmp.com/news/hong-kong/community/article/2125451/explainer-how-hong-kong-has-decades-been-magnet-refugees.

Clairmont, Nicholas. "'Those Who Do Not Learn History Are Doomed To Repeat It.' Really?" Big Think. September 7, 2020. Retrieved from: https://bigthink.com/culture-religion/those-who-do-not-learn-history-doomed-to-repeat-it-really/.

Dikotter, Frank. *The Cultural Revolution: A People's History, 1962–1976*. New York: Bloomsbury Publishing, 2016.

Eliot, T.S. "Little Gidding," *Four Quartets*, 1943.

Felitti, Vincent J. "The Relation Between Adverse Childhood Experiences and Adult Health: Turning Gold into Lead." *The Permanente Journal* 6, no. 1 (2002).

Finley, James. "Dialogue 3: The Ascent of Mount Carmel." *Turning to the Mystics* [podcast]. Center for Action and Contemplation. April 26, 2021. https://cac.org/podcasts/dialogue-3-the-ascent-of-mount-carmel/.

———. Lecture at Living School Intensive. Santa Monica, CA. February 2020.

"Forbidden City." *Encyclopedia Britannica*. Retrieved August 2, 2020. https://www.britannica.com/topic/Forbidden-City.

Frankl, Viktor. *Man's Search for Meaning: An Introduction to Logotherapy.* New York: Simon & Schuster/Touchstone, 1984.

Gerdemann, Jon (Director). *Joy Makers* (Motion Picture). Threesixzero Productions Pte Ltd., China, 2019.

Gentsch A, Kuehn E. "Clinical Manifestations of Body Memories: The Impact of Past Bodily Experiences on Mental Health." *Brain Sciences*. 12, no.5 (May 3, 2022): 594. https://doi.org/10.3390/brainsci12050594.

Girard, René. *The Scapegoat.* Boston: Johns Hopkins University Press, 1986.

Greenson, Thadeus. "Betty Chinn." *Eureka Times-Standard*. October 18, 2008.

———. "'A modern mountain man' Friends struggle to reconcile James James' violent end with the peaceful man they knew." *Eureka Times-Standard*. September 16, 2013.

———. "Betty Chinn: Activist." *North Coast Journal*. August 29, 2019.

———. "Chesbro names Betty Chinn for annual Woman of the Year honor." *Eureka Times-Standard*. February 28, 2010.

———. "Holiday season special with Betty Chinn." *Eureka Times-Standard*. November 17, 2009.

———. "St. Joseph lends Betty Chinn a helping hand." *Eureka Times-Standard*. May 3, 2009.

———. "'You are loved': Betty Chinn and volunteers ensure first day of school is special for homeless youths." *Eureka Times-Standard*. August 21, 2009.

Halliday, Jon, and Jung Chang. *Mao: The Unknown Story*. United Kingdom: Knopf, 2005.

He, Huifeng. "Forgotten stories of the great escape to Hong Kong across the Shenzhen border." *South China Morning Post,* January 13, 2013. https://www.scmp.com/news/china/article/1126786/forgotten-stories-huge-escape-hong-kong.

High, Anna. "'Non-Legal' Orphanages and the Chinese State." China Development Brief. October 10, 2013. https://chinadevelopmentbrief.org/reports/non-legal-orphanages-and-the-chinese-state/.

"Hong Kong: National security arrests over social media posts violate freedom of expression." Amnesty International. July 17, 2020. https://www.amnesty.org/en/latest/news/2020/07/hong-kong-national.

"Hong Kong's New Security Law: Why it Scares People." BBC News. July 1, 2020. https://www.bbc.com/news/world-asia-china-53256034.

Houston, Will. "King sentenced to over 18 years in state prison for crossbow killing." *Eureka Times-Standard*. July 7, 2014.

Introvigne, Massimo. "Fengqiao Experience: The CCP Revives a Maoist Terror Strategy." *Bitter Winter.* August 13, 2022. https://bitterwinter.org/fengqiao-experience-the-ccp-revives-a-maoist-terror-strategy/.

Jicai, Feng. *Ten Years of Madness: Oral Histories of China's Cultural Revolution.* San Francisco: China Books and Periodicals, 1996.

———. *Voices from the Whirlwind: An Oral History of the Chinese Cultural Revolution.* Translated by Cathy Silber. New York: Random House, 1991.

Jimmerson, Julie. "Female Infanticide in China: An Examination of Cultural and Legal Norms." *UCLA Pacific Basin Law Journal* 8, no. 1 (1990). https://escholarship.org/uc/item/80n7k798.

Johnson, Ian. *The Souls of China; The Return of Religion After Mao.* New York: Pantheon Books, 2017.

"Kaiping Diaolou and Villages." UNESCO World Heritage Convention. June 29, 2007. https://whc.unesco.org/en/list/1112.

Kumar, Anagha Bangalore, Huma Shamim, and Umashankar Nagaraju. "Premature Graying of Hair." *International Journal of Trichology* 10, no.5 (2018): 198–203.

Lentz, Mary Thibodeaux. "In Person: Second helping." *U.S. Catholic 75*, no. 6 (June 2010): 35–36.

Levine, Peter A. *Trauma and Memory: Brain and Body in a Search for the Living Past: A Practical Guide for Understanding and Working with Traumatic Memory.* Berkeley: North Atlantic Books, 2015.

Levine, Peter A. *Waking the Tiger: Healing Trauma.* Berkeley: North Atlantic Books, 1997.

McPhate, Mike. "California Today: A One-Woman Lifeline for Eureka's Homeless." *The New York Times.* October 25, 2016.

Mitchell, R. Scott, and Sofia Borges. *Give Me Shelter: Architecture Takes on the Homeless Crisis.* San Francisco: ORO Editions, 2018.

Mossman, Sue Y Lee. Unpublished interview. May 14, 2020.

———. Fundraising letter for shower facility. 2009.

Mungello, D. E. *Drowning Girls in China: Female Infanticide since 1650.* Lanham, MD: Rowman & Littlefield, 2008.

Newell, Roger. Unpublished communications. June 30, 2020.

Nouwen, Henri. *The Wounded Healer: Ministry in Contemporary Society.* New York: Doubleday Image Books, 1979.

O'Neel, B.K. "Questions Remain in California Priest's Tragic Slaying." *The Catholic World Report.* January 16, 2014.

Palmer, Parker J. *On The Brink of Everything: Grace, Gravity, and Getting Old.* Oakland: Berrett-Koehler, 2018.

Pomeroy, Caroline, Cynthia J. Thomson, and Melissa M. Stevens. *California's North Coast Fishing Communities Historical Perspective and Recent Trends: Eureka Fishing Community Profile.* UC San Diego: California Sea Grant College Program. November 2011.

"Resolution on Certain Questions in the History of Our Party since the Founding of the People's Republic of China," Wilson Center Digital Archive. Translation from *Beijing Review* 24, no. 27 (July 6, 1981).

———. "Prayer in Captivity." *Daily Meditations.* Center for Action and Contemplation. April 22, 2020.

Rohr, Richard. "Prayer in Captivity," *Daily Meditations*, Center for Action and Contemplation, April 22, 2020.

Ruoxi, Chen. *The Execution of Mayor Yin.* Bloomington: Indiana University Press, 2004.

Schoenhals, Michael. *China's Cultural Revolution, 1966-1969: Not a Dinner Party*. Armonk, NY: M.E. Sharpe Incorporated, 1996.

Schukwing, H. (2002). *Kaiping Diaolou*. China, 92.

Sittser, Gerald Lawson. *A Grace Disguised: How the Soul Grows Through Loss*. Grand Rapids, MI: Zondervan Publishing House, 1995.

Smit, Jan Olav. Pope Pius XII. London & Dublin: Burns, Oates, & Washbourne, 1951.

Solzhenitsyn, Aleksandr. *The Gulag Archipelago 1918–1956*. New York: HarperCollins, 2002.

Song, Yongyi. "Chronology of Mass Killings during the Chinese Cultural Revolution (1966-1976)." SciencesPo. Mass Violence and Resistance – Research Network. August 25, 2011. https://www.sciencespo.fr/mass-violence-war-massacre-resistance/en/document/chronology-mass-killings-during-chinese-cultural-revolution-1966-1976.html.

———. "What is the Chinese Cultural Revolution?" CSUSB Modern China Lecture Series. Los Angeles, CA. April 18, 2017.

Spence, Jonathan. *Mao Zedong: A Life*. New York: Penguin Books, 2006.

Stewart, Ian. "Chinese Refugees Swim Across a Perilous Bay to Hong Kong." *The New York Times*. June 22, 1972. https://www.nytimes.com/1972/06/22/archives/chinese-refugees-swim-across-a-perilous-bay-to-hong-kong.html.

———. "Flow of Refugees to Hong Kong from Mainland China Is Rising." *The New York Times*. September 12, 1971. https://www.nytimes.com/1971/09/12/archives/flow-of-refugees-to-hong-kong-from-mainland-china-is-rising.html.

Tan, Hecheng. *The Killing Wind: A Chinese County's Descent into Madness During the Cultural Revolution*. Translated by Stacy Mosher and Guo Jian. New York: Oxford University Press, 2017.

"The Cultural Revolution, 50 Years On. It Was the Worst of Times." *The Economist*. May 14, 2016. https://www.economist.com/china/2016/05/14/it-was-the-worst-of-times.

Torgan, Allie. "A horrific childhood in China inspires a crusade against homelessness." CNN Heroes. CNN. October 4, 2018. https://www.cnn.com/2018/10/04/us/cnnheroes-betty-chinn-betty-kwan-chinn-homeless-foundation/index.html.

Tutu, Desmond. *The Book of Forgiving.* New York: HarperCollins, 2014.

van der Kolk, Bessel. *The Body Keeps Score: Brain, Mind, and Body in the Healing of Trauma.* New York: Penguin Books, 2014.

VanderKlippe, Nathan. "Suppressed records revealed 50 years after China's Cultural Revolution," *The Globe and Mail.* May 15, 2016 (updated 2018). https://www.theglobeandmail.com/news/world/suppressed-records-revealed-50-years-after-chinas-cultural-revolution/article30028854/.

Wang, Hansi Lo. "Chinese-American Descendants Uncover Forged Family Histories." Morning Edition. NPR. December 17, 2013. https://www.npr.org/sections/codeswitch/2013/12/17/251833652/chinese-american-descendants-uncover-forged-family-history.

Wang, Youqin. *Victims of the Cultural Revolution: An Investigative Account of Persecution, Imprisonment and Murder.* Hong Kong: Kaifang Magazine Press, 2004.

Wang, Y.C. "Sun Yat-Sen, Chinese Leader." *Encyclopedia Britannica.* Updated November 8, 2022. https://www.britannica.com/biography/Sun-Yat-Sen.

Welsford, John. *Backyard Boatbuilder: How to Build Your Own Wooden Boat.* Auckland, NZ: Reed Books, 1999.

Wen, Chihua. *The Red Mirror: Children of China's Cultural Revolution.* Boulder, CO: Westview Press, 1995.

Wong, Kent. *Swimming to Freedom: My Escape from China and the Cultural Revolution.* New York: Abrams Press, 2021.

Wong, Paul T.P. *Autobiography: A Lifelong Search For Meaning: Lessons on Virtue, Grit, and Faith.* March 20, 2017. http://www.drpaulwong.com/hong-kong-a-haven-for-chinese-refugees/.

Wong, Tak-kan. "Last time it snowed in Hong Kong." Hong Kong Observatory. https://www.hko.gov.hk/en/education/climate/general-climatology/00247-last-time-it-snowed-in-hong-kong.html.

Yiwu, Liao. *God Is Red: The Secret Story of How Christianity Survived and Flourished in Communist China.* New York: HarperCollins, 2011.

Yu, Verna. "'Enemy of the people' historian Song Yongyi gives as good as he gets." *South China Morning Post*. February 19, 2013. https://www.scmp.com/news/china/article/1153447/enemy-people-historian-song-yongyi-gives-good-he-gets.

Zheng, Yi. *Scarlet Memorial: Tales of Cannibalism in Modern China*. Boulder, CO: Westview Press, 1996.

Zimbardo, Philip. *The Lucifer Effect: Understanding How Good People Turn Evil*. New York: Random House, 2007.

———. "The psychology of evil." TED Talks. 2008. https://www.ted.com/talks/philip_zimbardo_the_psychology_of_evil.

Zolbert, Aristide R., Astri Suhrke, and Sergio Aguayo. *Escape From Violence: Conflict and the Refugee Crisis in the Developing World*. United Kingdom: Oxford University Press, 1989.

Albert, Eleanor. "Christianity in China." Council on Foreign Relations. Updated October 11, 2018. https://www.cfr.org/backgrounder/christianity-china.

Branigan, Tania. "China's Great Famine: the true story." *The Guardian*. January 1, 2013. https://www.theguardian.com/world/2013/jan/01/china-great-famine-book-tombstone.

Buckley, Chris, and Austin Ramzy. "'Absolutely No Mercy': Leaked Files Expose How China Organized Mass Detentions of Muslims." The Xinjiang Papers. *The New York Times*. November 16, 2019. https://www.nytimes.com/interactive/2019/11/16/world/asia/china-xinjiang-documents.html.

Coale, Ansley J., and Judith Banister. "Five Decades of Missing Females in China." *Proceedings of the American Philosophical Society* 140, no. 4 (1996): 421–50. http://www.jstor.org/stable/987286.

"Factbox: China's 2010 Census." *Reuters*. April 28, 2011. https://www.reuters.com/article/us-china-census-factbox/factbox-chinas-2010-census-idUSTRE73R0XM20110428.

Falkenheim, Victoria, Chang Chen-tung, and Yeung Yue-man. "Guangdong Province." *Encyclopedia Britannica*. Updated September 22, 2022. https://www.britannica.com/place/Guangdong.

Gunia, Amy. "Prison Sentence for Pastor Shows China Feel Threatened by Spread of Christianity, Experts Say." January 2, 2020. *TIME*. https://time.com/5757591/wang-yi-prison-sentence-china-christianity/.

Johnson, Ian. "Who Killed More: Hitler, Stalin or Mao?" *The New York Review*. February 5, 2018. https://www.nybooks.com/online/2018/02/05/who-killed-more-hitler-stalin-or-mao/.

Liao, Yiwu. *God Is Red: The Secret Story of How Christianity Survived and Flourished in Communist China*. New York: Harper Collins, 2011.

Livingston, Gretchen. "Without One Child Policy China Still Might Not See Baby Boom, Gender Balance." Pew Research Center. November 20, 2015. https://www.pewresearch.org/fact-tank/2015/11/20/will-the-end-of-chinas-one-child-policy-shift-its-boy-girl-ratio/.

Rudolph, Barbara. "Unspeakable Crimes." *Time Magazine*. January 18, 1993. https://content.time.com/time/magazine/article/0,9171,160807,00.html.

Tang, Edmond, and Jean-Paul Weist. *The Catholic Church in China: Perspectives*. Eugene, OR: Wipf and Stock, 2013.

Thurston, Anne F. "In a Chinese Orphanage." *The Atlantic*. April 1996. https://www.theatlantic.com/magazine/archive/1996/04/in-a-chinese-orphanage/376563/.

Wang, Youqin. "Student Attacks Against Teachers: The Revolution of 1966." *Issues & Studies* 37, no.2 (March/April 2001): 29–79.

Zhao, Qigang. "Chinese Mythology in the Context of Hydraulic Society." *Asian Folklore Studies* 48, no. 2 (1989): 231–246.

Karen is a fourth generation Californian, born in the San Francisco Bay Area. She received a B.A. in Literature from Westmont College, an M.A. in Theology and Counseling from Fuller Seminary, and a Ph.D. in Clinical Psychology from the California School of Professional Psychology. She practiced as a clinical psychologist in California, Scotland, and Switzerland before moving with her family to Eureka, CA, where she practiced for 25 years and occasionally taught as an adjunct at what is now Cal Poly Humboldt. She and her husband have two grown and married children, four grandchildren, and live in the Redwoods of Northern California next door to their son, daughter-in-law and three of their grandchildren.